Lament
of the Dead
Psychology after Jung's Red Book

Lament
of the Dead
Psychology after
Jung's Red Book

JAMES HILLMAN &
SONU SHAMDASANI

W. W. NORTON & COMPANY

NEW YORK   LONDON

Lament of the Dead: Psychology after Jung's *Red Book*
James Hillman and Sonu Shamdasani

Printed in the United States of America

First Norton edition 2013

Book design and composition by Laura Lindgren

The text of this book is composed in Fleischman.

Manufactured by Courier Westford

Library of Congress Cataloging-in-Publication Data

Hillman, James.
 Lament of the dead : psychology after Jung's Red book / James Hillman
and Sonu Shamdasani. — First edition.
    pages cm
 Includes index.
  ISBN 978-0-393-08894-6 (hardcover)
 1. Jung, C. G. (Carl Gustav), 1875–1961. Liber novus.
 2. Jungian psychology. I. Shamdasani, Sonu, 1962– II. Title.
  BF109.J8H55 2013
  150.19'54—dc23   2013009451

W. W. Norton & Company, Inc.
500 Fifth Avenue
New York, N.Y. 10110
www.wwnorton.com

W. W. Norton & Company, Ltd.
Castle House, 75/76 Wells Street
London W1T 3QT

1 2 3 4 5 6 7 8 9 0

Contents

Preface

In October 2009, James Hillman and I commenced a series of conversations taking as their point of departure C. G. Jung's newly published Red Book. In April 2010 we held a public dialogue, at the invitation of the Hammer Museum in Los Angeles, California. In the following autumn and summer we continued discussions in Connecticut and New York. This book arises from the transcriptions of those conversations. Recurring motifs and themes taken up from different angles have been retained. We both went over the text, finalizing the manuscript before his death in the fall of 2011. I added endnotes for the sources of the works referred to. Subsequent revision has been restricted to copy editing.

Sonu Shamdasani

Lament
of the Dead

Psychology after
Jung's Red Book

I

Los Angeles

FIRST CONVERSATION

JAMES HILLMAN: I was reading about this practice that the ancient Egyptians had of opening the mouth of the dead.[1] It was a ritual and I think we don't do that with our hands. But opening the *Red Book* seems to be opening the mouth of the dead.

SONU SHAMDASANI: It takes blood. That's what it takes. The work is Jung's "Book of the Dead." His descent into the underworld, in which there's an attempt to find the way of relating to the dead. He comes to the realization that unless we come to terms with the dead we simply cannot live, and that our life is dependent on finding answers to their unanswered questions.

JH: *Their* unanswered questions.

SS: We think we're posing the questions but we're not. The dead are animating us.

JH: But the questions . . . Jung says there that we think the figures we uncover in our dreams or in active imagination are the result of us, but he says we are the result of them. Our life should be derived from them. We just think of it wrong. We think whatever comes to us comes to us as something leftover from, as Freud said, *Tagesrest,* the residues of the day, images that are composite stuff, garbage from life. But Jung is saying these figures come to us in our dreams and even our thoughts derive from these figures, so the task would be uncovering the figures, which seems to be what the *Red Book* does. He allows the figures to speak, to show themselves. He even encourages them to.

SS: Descending into his own depths he finds images that, in a sense, have preceded him. It is a descent into human ancestry.

JH: Good.

SS: It is the ancestors. It is the dead. This is no mere metaphor. This is no cipher for the unconscious or something like that. When he talks about the dead he means the dead. And they're present in images. They still live on.

JH: When I was doing therapy, back in another period of history, I always tried to escape the parents, which was the story that the person always wanted to tell me—what their mother did and what their father did. You notice Jung hasn't a lot to say about them anywhere in the *Red Book*.

SS: There's no "Mommy, Daddy, me," as Gilles Deleuze and Félix Guattari would put it.[2]

JH: But to go and ask people about their grandparents and their great-grandparents and imagining all their great-grandparents sitting down at a table. That would be eight people. Could they eat the same food? Could they talk the same language? Could they even sit with each other? But the ancestors in the book—see the reason being that it shows the enormous complexities in human nature and the incompatibilities in human nature. And the fact that your actual parents whom you think caused everything are actually the result of those tremendous incompatibilities themselves. It frees them up too. But, in this story, in this book, the ancestors are more than his personal eight great-grandparents. What about, when you use the word "ancestors" there, how do you use it? Or how does Jung use it?

SS: Well, the question is, who are the dead? And this is a question that he poses and ponders within this text. There is a sense in which, in the broadest scope, it is the dead of human history. We are at an epoch where the dead outnumber the living. There is this one level of an anonymous stream of the dead, of the weight of human history and what it has left that we have to come to terms with. At another level it becomes more specific. Certain figures come out more prominently, differentiate themselves from the stream and present themselves in specific figures.

JH: They present themselves as figures of a historic moment, or of a historic period at least, but they're not historic figures. Like Vico, who spoke to his historic figures. He had busts of them and he spoke to them and they were actual figures—Grotius and I forget all of them.[3] There were four. And Jung had Voltaire in his study, didn't he? But Voltaire's not in the *Red Book*. What I mean is the history, the historic figures are not actual. He's not in a dialogue with philosophers of the past.

SS: Well, some. *Zarathustra* is there. Nietzsche is there. Goethe is there. So, in some instances, you have this reverberation of this specific legacy of thinkers, and then the troop of Anabaptists bursts into the kitchen one day saying they're just off to pray at the holiest of places. Jung asked to go along and they say he can't go because he's got a body.[4] And what's striking about this episode is Anabaptism was a movement that originated in the sixteenth century in Jung's neighborhood. The first adult baptisms, which were a prominent feature of the Anabaptist movement, took place down the road at Zollikon. So there is a sense of specific historical figures emerging as well.

JH: And they emerge. They were not as the result of his reading. Because you said the other day that his immersion in the reading of texts written by traditional theologians and writers and agnostics and other writings that he read eventually became part of the language he uses for saying what he wants to say.

SS: I think it fired his imagination.

JH: It fired his imagination, yes.

SS: A mode of utterance. A mode of fantasizing in a mythical and epic manner. In a ritualistic manner. This language, initially I'd say, intoxicated him.

JH: So it also then became the language that was adequate for what he wanted. It was the rhetoric that allowed him to express what he wanted to express. It's not just that they influenced him, it suited him or it suited what he wanted to say.

SS: It also, in a way to take it back to what we were saying earlier, suited the characters. This was a language that was appropriate to what emerged. And at certain times, he indicates later, he felt uncomfortable. This was something forced upon him. This was not his normal tongue. But he was forced into utterance in a specific way that was adequate to the task. There was no other language that was appropriate.

JH: When did he first come on this language? Was it in the *Seven Sermons* or was it earlier?

SS: I take it to be in the summer of 1914. The first layer of the text, running from October of 1913 through to February, where he engages in introspective elaboration of his fantasies, the method that he subsequently calls active imagination, is not an elevated language. It's a precise depiction of what transpires. He maintains in that what I call a fidelity to the event.

JH: Fidelity to the event.

SS: Accurate notation, dates, precision, indicating that something of significance is taking place. There is no attempt to fictionalize it. It's quite fantastic but it is real.

JH: And he is recording.

SS: He is recording it.

JH: I wanted to ask you about that. Does he record as it happens? Or does he record after he's had the dialogues? Because when I did active imagination myself long ago most of it was done as it happened. So it was a writing, in a way. Some of it was not. Some of it was a conversation, interior, and then I would write it—recapture it—by writing.

SS: This is one of the imponderable questions of which I've hit my head against the wall for many a year now in that it's hard to make a decision on this. Certain segments of the text give the sense that he sees a dramatic sequence and then notes it down, whereas certain other segments of the text appear to unfold in the writing.

JH: Unfold in the writing as a flowing dialogue.

SS: Yes. Or there are certain statements that I like. There's one point where he says, "I've run out of tobacco so I can't write anymore."

JH: That's good.

SS: My intuition leans to this as a writing experience, but again you can't be sure about this. Just looking at the materiality of the text suggests to me as a writer that he's writing this out.

JH: Yes. But he does report dreams.

SS: Well actually very few and that's one striking element of the text—my reading of this is that the dreams and the fantasies are separate layers. There are very few dreams noted, and there's also very surprisingly little interplay between his dreams during this period and the fantasies that unfold.

JH: So he doesn't take a figure from a dream and begin to work with that dream, that figure.

SS: No, if anything sometimes the opposite occurs. Characters from his fantasies then reemerge in the dream.

JH: Ah. That's interesting.

SS: This is the stream of imagery that he is then enabling to present itself and that he's engaged with. There's an active engagement here.

JH: But what are we to do now? What are we to do with this extraordinary thing? What are we to do in psychology? So many people have been in psychology or been in Jungian analysis or been Jungians or engaged in this work of his or results of the work. What do we do now? Because it seems to me those eighteen volumes of his have to be reconsidered—they don't seem to be in the *Red Book.*

SS: I've sometimes thought that if a fire broke out what text would I take? This is the text of Jung that I would take. And I would leave the rest. You can reconstruct so much of what is essential in what is to come in the rest of his works from this text.

JH: What is essential.

SS: It's by no means the whole in the sense that Jung is a polyphonic writer. He continues with conventional theorizing. He gets involved in typology and psychological energetics. He's got many pots on the go at one time. But when you read this text and look at the works that come after, you see certain places where it's as if the seams are exposed. Or that this underground stream is closer to the surface. It comes up.

JH: Yes.

SS: And one thing that struck me about this was that a number of copies of this text were in circulation—were in, you could say, undercover circulation. I'd assumed through reading your work that you had read a copy and I actually would have put money on it.

JH: You would have lost.

SS: Now why did I think that?

JH: Maybe the parts of Jung that I fell for were those places that had to do with the images, not with the concepts, the statements that struck me as revelatory, you know the absolute importance of fantasy, the voices, the emphasis on active imagination as therapy. But more than that it's something . . . I guess it's partly because of a skeptical disbelief in conceptual terms for psychic life. For example, I often say don't use the word "ego." I've never seen one. I've never seen an "ego." I don't know what we're talking about. And that goes for an enormous number of these terms that have become psychology, so psychology for me had something else to it and I found that something else in what you call the seams in his work.

SS: Well, this is Jung without concepts. You find Jung expressing the essence of his activities, tasks, his oeuvre, without a single conceptual term. There is no archetype. There's no unconscious, and he gets by quite fine without it. In fact, he manages to express himself in a more fitting and particular way.

JH: So when you save that book from the fire and let the others go, evidently that's the implication of your figment there, a lot of the concepts would go. Where would we be in psychology if the concepts are gone?

SS: My sense in that those concepts were a makeshift. They're an attempt to try to translate as much as he felt he could get away with to the medico-scientific audience of his time.

JH: Well he defends them too. Sometimes he says a concept in German is a *Begriff* and a *Begriff* means to be able to grip something, to take hold of it.

SS: Yes, and there's a utility in it. But there's also a sense of a traducement, which contrasts with that which he engages within this text. He speaks about words. He speaks about concepts as an attempt to tame the incomprehensible, the chaos. And in this text he tries to do away with that as much as possible, to confront the immediacy of his own experience.

JH: But there is a mode of the confrontation that in some way articulates it? Transcribes it? Paints it? So concepts are not the only way of taking hold.

SS: No. By no means. What he engages in is a lyrical elaboration, an evocation—

JH: Did you say lyrical? That's very interesting.

SS: A lyrical elaboration. An evocation. An attempt to find fitting expressions so that the images resonate. They're able to speak. So to take one example, there's one of the chapters in which he meets a one-eyed vagabond, a desolate figure, who ends up just dying in the night.[5] In his reflections on this he speaks about the destitute, the beggar who wants to enter in, who wants acceptance with him and comes to think that he had cast aside his beggarliness, and he had not accepted himself because there was this desolate vagabond that he had thrown away. He doesn't attempt to translate it. For instance to call it, using his later language, the "shadow." He speaks about it in terms of beggarliness, destitution. He allows the metaphorical word to open up and that's what I think is most compelling about this second layer of lyrical elaboration—when he allows it to echo.

JH: So he's really using the language of literature or drama or poetry. He's using descriptive or concrete words about what's going on in the psyche, not second-level abstractions.

SS: Yes.

JH: Yes. But we have, when we do psychology, we psychologists, we are taught abstractions, systems of abstractions. Not only that, we read Jung in translation in English. It's not even what Jung wrote. And somehow this must create maybe a six or a seven tremor in the underground.

SS: It does. We can maybe hear it underneath us. "Psychology" is also a word that does not appear in this text.

JH: Well, yes. It didn't appear—I mean really appear—until the beginning of the nineteenth century.

SS: But he's not using it in this work.

JH: And he knew psychology and he knew psychiatry and maybe at second level, third level he says something about the events but not the word "psychology."

SS: Psychology is what he is doing in his day world.

JH: Yes.

SS: This is a private text initially, although it's written for others. He's working on it for publication. But it's an elaboration of a personal cosmology which is not conceptual. It presents the framework in which he refound orientation and meaning in his life. And the question is that that wasn't provided to him by his concepts. His concepts were of utility to others and that was part of his, you could say, physician's task—to provide something for others that would give them orientation when they faced the dark nights in their own underworlds.

JH: But he didn't use that on his own.

SS: No, it's not the primary language. And there's a problem that enters when one confuses the two. So to read this text and to translate one language into the other is to traduce it. He could have used these words had he so wished.

JH: So that leaves open for us who read it to discover another way of speaking psychology. It's closer to the phenomena as they appear.

SS: There are the heights and the depths. There is not the conscious and the unconscious in this text. There are the powers of the depths. There are the principles of the depths.

JH: And their voices.

SS: And their voices, which he hears.

JH: Yes. So how would we work if we put those eighteen volumes aside for a moment and the concepts in them and the systems and the typologies and the diagrams and so on—we put that aside—how would we practice a psychology? Or do we disband psychology?

SS: It will be over at four p.m. Call a day on it.

JH: That's it. Thank you!

SS: I think one has to look first at how psychological concepts are actually used and was developed in a task to complete the scientific revolution. The notion was psychology was to be the master science that would underpin all the other sciences. Well, this clearly didn't work. We've got as many psychologies almost as there are people. And the one thing that I think all psychologists have in common is that they don't agree about anything, apart from that they use the word "psychology." So you have to ask is this a science? Clearly, a lot of productive work has gone on under this enterprise.

JH: Oh yes, yes.

SS: And my sense is that—

JH: I say this "oh yes, oh yes" to dismiss going further into it.

SS: I realize you've written a few books with the word "psychology" in it.

JH: Yes.

SS: Within psychology, these concepts are actually already used as images. The frameworks for understanding have given rise to new forms of life themselves. They may not be the richest forms of expression but that's how they're actually employed. So in one sense it's not really a need to develop a new language but to look at the metaphorical ways or to look at the uses to which language is employed. It's a type of anthropology of psychology.

JH: The uses in which language is already being employed. This doesn't strike a happy note with me because I hear the way that psychology uses its language as *apotropaic*—as a way of covering the fundamental anxiety that we don't know anything really about psyche. And so we have developed systems that ban the demons or that ban the unknown, which the psyche remains as. Jung says again and again about how little we know what we're talking about.

SS: That's an example then of what a type of anthropology would show if these concepts are used as you say, as bulwarks against the unknowable that breaks in and sweeps us under anyway.

JH: Well, the permanent sense that out there we're not on solid ground. We don't know what we're talking about. We don't *know* what we're talking about.

SS: Or we are part of what we are talking about, in the sense of the problem that animated Jung, of reflexivity. There is no outside because it is ourselves that is the question here. I think that—back to this question of the uses—Jung does see a therapeutic function in conceptual language in the sense that, for some people, without this there is madness. It does have some utility.

JH: So it is apotropaic.

SS: It is. But I don't think in his own life he actually used it in the sense of this was not the language that was closest to him.

JH: Not just that. He had another mode of keeping the madness or the engulfment away. He had his daily life.

SS: That was tremendously significant for him.

JH: Yes, so it's not that he spent twenty-four hours in a day with that. He didn't need the concepts as a bulwark because he had the daily life. He had his practice. He had his official duties. He had his family. He had so on. So that becomes another mode of opening the mouth of the dead if you have this world around you into which you can go and sleep.

SS: He gave himself to the everyday. Another aspect of this text is a reappreciation of the banal, of what he as an intellectual had shunned, of turning back to the smallest things,[6] of realizing that the ultimate truths were not necessarily remote but could be recovered in the simplest of pleasures.

JH: He talks about that—actually of "joy."[7] Well, we haven't really solved it. We haven't really discovered how to go on talking and practicing what's called psychology, even defining it, even confirming what we know. And yet what you called our epistemological insecurity is fundamental. That is, we don't really know what we're doing. If that's the case, then we have to articulate another . . . I still think we have to find other forms. You mentioned one already. The lyrical . . . what was it?

SS: Elaboration.

JH: Lyrical elaboration, which suggests dramatic, aesthetic, poetic, artistic, painterly, or whatever, forms—artwork—forms of elaborating what the dead want to say.

SS: To me it's a question of abandoning the notion that psychology is a quest for knowledge, to take up your question in another way. And you say if after one hundred years they haven't agreed about anything, well, they aren't going to and it seems to me a fair enough assumption to draw, and it's given it enough time, and one asks what actually has the enterprise been about? It has to my mind functioned as a means of providing individuals a form of articulating their experiences. It has provided certain languages, possibly in some cases deficient, in some cases more enriching, which bring fuller articulation to their experiences.

JH: But there could be better lyricism.

SS: There could be but also within that, if one accepts that, it is no longer the master key that unlocks all the other languages, but is simply one modality among others.

JH: And so you become, then, a member of this or that tribe within the giant system because you're using the same language.

SS: Yes, and what that language can do is enable individuals to refind a way through the chaos, of bearing their experience.

JH: And Jung, in a sense, offered such a language. Instead of talking about the bottommost and the beggarly and the derelict, he invented the figure of the shadow, the personified concept of shadow. So he's trying to do it, it's as close, in a way.

SS: It is as close, but also with one caveat, in that he didn't want to turn people into Jungians. He didn't expect his scientific apparatus, which is how he saw it, as something that provided meaning to people's lives. He saw the whole enterprise as about enabling individuals to refind their own language, develop their own cosmologies. And, as he says, he eschewed using concepts within his therapeutic practice. If someone comes in talking about spirits, he talks about spirits. I take that very seriously—and it's borne out by accounts I found in diaries and letters of his practice—to enable individuals to articulate their own linguistic worlds.

JH: And not translating.

SS: Not translating. So the conceptual language is there as part of his scientific enterprise, when he's reflecting on this and trying to constitute a science.

JH: When he wants to talk to the medical side.

SS: But his practice is quite different, and his self-experimentation, his own self-investigation, is quite different.

JH: This would indicate then that each person, each individual, would use the language that is given by the figures that he or she deals with or confronts or appear.

SS: Yes.

JH: So we each become, in a sense, a poet of our own psyches. But there's a hang-up there, because there's some pretty bad poets. Meaning, you know, inarticulate, limited, sentimental, untruthful, whatever. What about that? Would there be better and worse languages or better and worse formulations?

SS: I think then that the task is one of valuation, in that not every language is on a par. To say that one is then looking, not in terms of a correspondence of truth, but looking at richer and fuller articulations and in terms of what furthers and enables life. As William James put it, in terms of pragmatism.[8] What enables an individual to live more fully?

JH: Yes. *Das wirkt.* Effective. What's effective or what enables a person to live more fully.

SS: I'm struck by the poet Blaise Cendrars commenting on first hearing Ellington and he says that this is not just a new music but a new reason for living.[9]

JH: That's lovely. There is an aesthetic aspect to this then.

SS: But also one that has, as Jung stressed, ethics in it. In the sense that he says the images came with a burden of responsibility. That he was given a boon, as he puts it. But they indicate what he subsequently had to earn and realize in life.[10] That's his engagement with his figures—he was engaged in this work regardless of whether he was working on it directly or not. When he's away from the book, he's trying to realize the book in actuality. He certainly was not wanting his own cosmology to be taken up by others, which is one aspect of the reticence to publish it. So he doesn't want individuals to have their own inner Izdubar or their own Ammonius.[11]

JH: He says that again and again. He says that so often about not teaching: "It is no teaching and no instruction that I give you. I give you news of one way of this man."[12] This man, him, "but not of your own way. My path is not your path. Woe betide those who live by way of examples."[13] It seems to me that is enormously important because otherwise this becomes a new Bible and then we have *Imitatio Dei*.

SS: But at the same time there's a tension in the work, in that he's still attempting to generalize, to find general principles from his fantasies and indicate that his fantasies didn't concern himself alone but—

JH: That's very important. These fantasies didn't concern himself alone. That goes back to the voices of the dead. There's collective strength, and collective message, a collective importance in what is coming up.

SS: Yes, and this to me is the unresolved tension in the work— between on the one hand *ecce homo*, that is, do not take me for what I'm not, and on the other hand who I am is someone who is attempting to provide something more generic, something that indicates the way of what is to come. Because in reflecting on himself, he does not come across at rock bottom his own personal biography, but it's an attempt to uncover the quintessentially human. These dialogues are not dialogues with his past, as you're indicating.

JH: No.

SS: But with the weight of human history.

JH: So you say this is an inherent tension in the book between what is his, personal—personal in the deepest sense of personal, not personal in the sense of his mother and his father and his loves and so on but personal in the root figures who come to him, to him only—and yet bringing something to him that is historical, collective, and in a way speaks to the zeitgeist.

SS: And also the question—which is posed I'd say initially in relation to his therapeutic practice because this is also what I call a collective experiment—is this also true of others and if so in what way?

JH: The work with, say, Christiana Morgan later in the *Visions* seminars would be establishing again that this is a process of the voices wanting the same things.[14]

SS: Or "you have that voice too." And the sense of trying to determine what is generic and what isn't. And this task of discrimination is what he spent the rest of his life engaged in. Yes, in some sense what happened to him was wholly particular but, in the other sense, it was universally human and that generates his project of the comparative study of the individuation process.

JH: Yes. So he examines *The Tibetan Book of the Dead, The Egyptian Book of the Dead*. He examines Ignatius of Loyola. He examines Kundalini yoga and so on and so forth as parallel experiments.[15]

SS: Yes, when he stops working on this and in the 1930s begins his alchemy copy books in which he's taking citations, principally from alchemical texts, also from other sources, and sometimes they're interspersed with references to some of his own images or his own dreams.[16]

JH: Oh yes, he actually published some of those pictures.

SS: Yes. And there's a sense in which in his study of symbolism, his own images are what he has at the back of his mind. He recognizes them elsewhere and that strikes him.

JH: Don't the voices themselves claim universality? Don't they speak in a prophetic voice at times and doesn't he struggle with that?

SS: Absolutely. That commences with his encounter with Elijah and reaches its apotheosis in his engagement with the figure of Philemon. Part of the critical work of understanding in which he engages is a differentiation of the voices, a disidentification.

JH: Disidentification?

SS: Yes. He realizes around about 1917 that the prophetic tone, the prophetic language in which he wrote the first two sections of the text were given to him by this figure of Philemon, in other words, there's a prophetic voice in him that is not himself.[17] The issue then is one of differentiating being instructed by it without identifying with it. He did have a real career choice. He could have set up shop like Rudolf Steiner around the corner in Dornach and said, "This is the new revelation." I mean, gurus are two a penny in Europe in the 1920s—prophets of the new age, competing for the same clientele. He could have done that. But what then is interesting, what makes Jung *Jung* is, in a certain sense, the fact that he doubts his own visions and is more interested in the vision-making function than simply proclamation.

JH: See, to my mind that's the psychologist.

SS: That's the reflexivity.

JH: That reflexivity of what's going on here. Hearing the content and then looking through, trying to see through just the content. So you're moving from the literal. But he does say when the voices speak to you, when the anything comes you must engage with them as literally as you can. And then the reflection is in another tone, in another mind-set. But the engagement has to be literal.

SS: And you find that in the first layer of the text, where he enters in these fantasies and fully engages with what transpired, he's initially genuinely shocked by what the figures say. And then the work of understanding is attempting to come to terms with it.

JH: What the figures say and what they do and what he's asked to do is pretty shocking, pretty horrible in some cases.

SS: It is and he's forced in his confrontation to encompass what he rejected in his life.

JH: But even things that are altogether human like cannibalism or something that's not just what he rejected in his own life but are part of the extension of humankind—what you mentioned earlier on. That this collective opening the mouth of the dead is to go back through human history so that this thing always has meaning beyond for him alone.

SS: Also it is an attempt to come to an affirmation of the fullness of life.

JH: The fullness of life.

SS: Including what is most horrific in it. It's a realization that if you rejected part of existence then you've rejected, in a way, all of it.

JH: And this had to do with coming to terms with Christianity too.

SS: Yes.

JH: Or Christianity as it had been put on him, let's say.

SS: Christianity had come to simply a partial affirmation of aspects of existence and left off much.

JH: In fact, it was part of why he had lost his soul, which is the way the book opens if I remember, the search for his soul.[18] That led to the Christian incompletion, that it wasn't enough or what he had received wasn't enough, or in fact was even oppressive.

SS: Yes, and one aspect that he comes to is precisely that it rejected the dead. In one of the sharpest statements in the book he states, "Not one item of the Christian law is abrogated, but instead we are adding a new one: accepting the lament of the dead."[19]

JH: To accept the lament of the dead. Now, you see why Jung gets attacked is because he does that. Karl Jaspers attacks him for being a demonologist—inviting all kinds of demons back in that Christ succeeded in banning.[20] "Get thee behind me, Satan."[21] Harrowed hell. You know, all of that suppression of the underworld is exactly where it all came back.

SS: It'd become in a certain sense demonic because—

JH: Well, if you live down there long enough, I would think, through the centuries, you become pretty demonic.

SS: That he is valuing what is there and not rejecting it in terms of something that should be discarded.

JH: Let me ask you now. You know the book, you've said this is the essential book. You can tell us what Jung did. And so we want to know now from you.

SS: You're not going to ask me about my personal life!

JH: What do we do now? Now that the book is out there and there's something in the contemporary collective that wants the book. Where you have gone all over people show up. I'm sure it's for you but it's also for the book.

SS: It is striking and compelling. And I think that, again, just with my historical temperament, I'd say in a few years' time people will look back and ask what was actually taking place.

JH: What temperament?

SS: Historical.

JH: Oh! Because I heard "hysterical" and I couldn't fit it to you.

SS: The reception of the work is striking, but it doesn't actually surprise me, given the vast hinterland of readership of Jung. And given that when you see the effects, you could say, of books with low Jung content, as in sort of alcohol-free beer and names of post-Jungian authors whose names I will not mention, something that was a hundred percent proof was bound to have an impact. This is Jung in his own voice. It's not Jung as people have pretended he is. It's not the man of fiction, of the biographers. It's not a counterfeit.

JH: We're going to the source.

SS: Yes, this is a man of flesh and blood, as Unamuno would have called it.[22] And it's not then to me surprising that this would have an effect. It seems to me that there is some parallelism at this historical juncture of this quest for validation of inner experience, the search for meaning in the broadest sense of the word, and an echo in the manner in which Jung engaged with his own figures—not with his concepts because that's not there. The public isn't being taken by his ideas as they've been portrayed but by his actual intense engagement with his own figures.

JH: And that would be speaking to the zeitgeist.

SS: In some way.

JH: That it is the loss of the dead in that sense. That is the collective symptom. The loss of the contact with the dead.

SS: And that presents itself through fantasy.

JH: So the sense that has been described now for maybe forty years—from Mitford and Becker,[23] of the denial of death, the fear of death, the culture that lives always into the future and into the forward and that the basic malaise of our culture is the denial of death—is being responded to by the book. Here, this is a way of connecting. This is a way of opening the door. In that sense, this is the revolutionary cure to the real disease of our culture—the denial of death. And denial more as repression and escape from, flight from.

SS: And how the dead mounted in the period while this book slept in the bank vaults. "We need the coldness of death to see clearly," he states, we cannot live in a genuine way without encountering that.[24] Which is also accepting responsibility for history. That to come to terms with not only who we are as individuals—

JH: But with the culture or the civilization, rather.

SS: And that's the task that Jung sets himself. When he reflects on the first world war, he speaks about it in terms of an inner complicity. We are all engaged in this. We are taking part in each murder.[25] What happens in the collective is also taking place within us.

JH: Yes.

SS: There is a coresponsibility with what is happening in the world. And the problem is how to recognize that.

JH: So that it isn't merely an inner journey.

SS: Paradoxically, it's a journey out. But to go out, he has to go in. There is no direct way to the world without plunging into his solitude. And it's only through that that he reconnects with the living.

JH: It may seem as if these are two distinct paths, or even stages. You first go in and then you come out with what used to be called the return or the descent from the mountain and so on. But I think there's something else there. It think it's more a matter of realizing that there is a porous permeability between the living and the dead. Between life and death. And the way we have set it up is that death and life are opposed and you must hold off death and it's the ultimate other, and you die alone, this sort of existential whatever. And it seems to me that this offers a completely different way of realizing that the day world is permeated with the other world—in all kinds of small ways, that they're always inner voices, that the dead are cautionary figures. That you are living with the dead. And what you think of as the way of life may be the way of more death. And the way of death may be the way of more livingness. That these are not necessarily alternatives or that first you do one and then you do the other.

SS: To use a word that comes to mind from the philosopher David Krell: life/death.[26] Jung indicates that the dead are under the eves of our roofs.[27]

JH: Yes, exactly, exactly.

SS: In close proximity. And what is called for is a shift in recognition. That they are already there.

JH: The realm of the dead is already there.

SS: Yes.

JH: We are already in the realm of the dead. That it isn't something other and distant or sudden or opposite.

SS: Yes, again to take up this point that if you think the questions that animate you haven't been set by you. When you think you have got your hand on the tiller, navigating your path, to actually take on board that someone else is actually spinning the wheel.

JH: Yes, the questions that occupy you have been handed to you. That's one of Jung's main thoughts, that one.

SS: Yes, you've been had. You're being used by the dead. And the sooner you realize that the better.

JH: And what do they want with me?

SS: Yes, but also to then reach a right relation which is not one of subservience.

JH: No, he struggles all the way through.

SS: The dead want to take you over. It is then a quite literal possession that is at play there. At risk there. But in a way it's only through recognizing their demands that one is actually able to separate out from them at the same time and regain one's independence.

JH: The idea of their being so close seems to me the important thing, you say, in the eves of the house. It's the living in the house, of *their* house, actually. I may be exaggerating this but I'm allowed to. And I think that is crucial—we're back to why the book and Jung are now important, or picked up, or alive. Something we need to recognize. Or are recognizing already just by going to the book.

SS: That just brought to mind a conversation I had with Franz Jung, Jung's son, at one point where he said he often heard his father knocking around the house still. He just accepted it. His presence was still there.

JH: Franz Jung lived in Jung's house after Jung died.

SS: At one point he said he had an anxious stranger come running to the door and say, I have an important communication to you from your father. He said that's not possible, I'm in contact with him every day. I just spoke to him half an hour ago!

JH: It would be a big change in this culture. See, I think people already know all of this. They have their synchronistic moments, they have their cautionary hunches and senses, and they have a no-no that comes up every so often and this is all part of the livingness close to another world.

SS: It was something that was a constant in my work on the text. I wasn't editing this for the living. I was editing it for the dead.

JH: So interesting. I used to go to Eranos and they'd ask and I'd say I'm talking to the dead. Every year I'd give a lecture there but I never thought I was talking to the audience. It was for the benefit of the dead, but it was also addressing the fact that perhaps only they could understand what I was trying to get at.

SS: I was presented with an unfinished manuscript corpus in which there were just an endless series of choices of how to present the work or indeed whether to present the work at all, such that if when I was asked to write reports on it for the Jung family I had to think, well, should this work come out. And at critical junctures I actually explicitly directed myself to the figures. And I was engaged working on the text and said, well, if you want to come out in the world this is the moment. And sometimes I thought why don't you give me more help? Suddenly I thought, okay, maybe I was appealing to the wrong character at such a juncture!

JH: Oh, I completely understand that. I think novelists have that question when they don't know what to do. They have to turn to the figures as to how to end this or how to move this or what do we do now? I mean, you can't do it alone.

SS: No, and the work, to use an expression that Jung uses, is the legacy of the dead. In the sense that it is completing an incomplete task of Jung. He struggled with this leviathan. He never finished.

JH: An incomplete task called Jung.

SS: Yes, or his incomplete task.

JH: Yes! Of course.

SS: Yes, so he never brought it to shore. It was too much for him. He left it to posterity as a message floating in a bottle. At a certain point it would come ashore. But he didn't know when. Now the question then that I had was Jung was clearly ambivalent about the publication and I think he still would be ambivalent today. I think he would have gone ballistic if he read the *New York Times* piece in September 2009. What I intended was to remain faithful to that ambivalence. I didn't want to resolve it. I wanted it to be such that if he was still ambivalent about its publication, he wouldn't be ambivalent about the *form* of its publication.

JH: That's very good.

SS: That was my task.

JH: Well, "the form of its publication" presents it as an object of careful, respectful elucidation without any interpretation. But it's elucidated through your footnotes. How many are there?

SS: I did count once. I think one and a half thousand or so.

JH: Yes. The form of the presentation gives it honor and a certain pedestal.

SS: I wasn't ever attempting to interpret the text, which I avoided. And many people can and will use this—particularly the images—as a Rorschach blob. But I intended to indicate the layering of the text so you could see the composition, because that belongs to the work, the psychological work of elaboration, the meditation on the images you see in the layering. And also to indicate the transformations with the subsequent contemporary and *Collected Works*, where you see the tension between the two languages being played out. And I think Jim Mairs of W. W. Norton has done a great thing making the book so heavy. This is not a book that will compete with BlackBerries and iPods on the commuter rails. This can't go to the beach.

JH: It's not summer reading.

SS: It's a work that requires one to make an easel for it. And you really need two copies. One open at the images and one at the text.

JH: We haven't talked about the images, you and I. Neither of us has wanted to talk about the images.

SS: I worked on the text for about four years before seeing all the images. And I'm glad I did it that way. Because you almost get the bends if you start with the images. You descend too quickly into the depths. Because the images come after the text, or the bulk of them. In a way, in terms of what we were talking about, the images are his attempt to continue the elaboration, the echoing of the text through the images, and they continue the narrative. They become self-standing in their own right.

JH: Some do. I think some are apotropaic in their own right. The mandala images, when you look at them awhile and go back to when Jung was in military service in 1917 and drew in his military notebook, sort of pencil mandalas, I think they're a way of—he says so himself—they're ways of making order. But the order seems to me to be defensive. And if you look at them some look like drawing of castle moats and walls. And they are so balanced and so different from the life of the text that I feel that to start with mandalas or be focused on mandalas is the wrong way around. It's imprisoning.

SS: I think that it's an important question. The question is how these images are viewed. And what I think is fascinating about seeing the sequence of the pencil images is that the critical element for me is not in an individual image but in the transit, in the transforms between the images. The images mutate.

JH: Oh, as they reshape.

SS: And that to me is the key. It's not in the individual images but in the transitus between them. And that's where a drama occurs. And yes there is a risk of closure, a risk of an endpoint. And what Jung realizes is that the mandala—it's not as if, okay, you've realized the "self," you can pack up now, we've reached an intense religious realization—because it is a religious experience for Jung. But he realizes he has to go back and get there another way in the form of a spiral, in other words, it's an approximation that never gets there. It's never complete. So in a certain sense he is taken by this and particularly with the mandala that he draws in 1927 after his Liverpool dream.[28] He talks about this as a vision of beauty without which his life would have lost meaning. Again, it's a very interesting expression.

JH: Oh for me very important, the sense of beauty.

SS: It's beauty which has provided an essential meaning for his whole existence. But he realizes he can't stay with it.

JH: Well beauty ever fades. That's what beauty does. It's not that he can't stay with it, it won't stay.

SS: It won't stay. He has to let it go so that it can reemerge. I don't think it becomes static. There is clearly that danger, and there is a danger of being trapped within it, of clinging to it, that he himself is grappling with.

JH: You've helped me with that because I've always found it being used defensively. Or, as you say, getting trapped in their weight and perfection. And holding all the demons within the walls. And those that don't get in are outside and so on but that, the transition between the images as they move, that, as you say, is the crucial way to look at them.

SS: It breaks up. It's just a momentary stasis that is only one stage in . . . I don't want to use the word "process," that's the wrong word, but in a sequence.

I want to return to the issue you indicated of personification because that plays an important part in your own work and that is what is most vividly enacted in this text.

JH: Oh absolutely. Maybe that's why you thought I'd read it.

SS: One reason.

JH. Because I use that in the first chapter of *Re-Visioning Psychology*, called "Personifying."[29] It seemed the essential. And then reading your notes I found that Jung had read—was it Staudenmaier?—who had thought that that was the best way of engaging what was then called the subliminal, the subconscious.[30] But it isn't that it's a method of engaging, it's that figures speak because they want to speak, as Mary Watkins said[31]; when you're writing a novel people start talking or when you're writing a play the people start talking because you're not talking. In fact, when you get ideas, they're our voices. And the voices eventually become figures. And that's the difference between concept and person. Once you're engaged with a personified figure the emotion is there, love is there, dislike, all kinds of emotional activity. Psychological activity with the voice or a person. But with the concept, what can you do? I can't do anything with "the shadow" until "the shadow" is figured as someone or something or some animal or place that's personified and we are then at work with each other. So there's probably more to the personification than even that because that implies it's a method whereas the figures in the *Red Book* appear as persons. And there's another one of the old psychoanalysts who said you can't love anything unless it's personified. Unless it appears in a personified form. In a way it is the beginning of loving the work that you're engaged with.

SS: I'm reminded of William James's statement in *The Principles of Psychology*, "Thought tends to personal form."[32] And what one finds present in this work is—I think it can be best characterized as a form of thinking in a dramatic form. That is how I characterize Jung's dialogues.

JH: That opens a big window. Because we've been talking in psychological and psychoanalytic language, even in Jung in the beginning, in psychodynamics. And as you said the other day the original work of Jung was to show that these myths—as in *Symbols of Transformation*[33]—were the depiction of the libido in mythical forms. So it was a psychodynamic unfolding but in actuality we should talk about psychodramatics. And if we talk about psychodramatics—I used that term somewhere long ago— it implies that we're in a different realm of a different God. We're in the realm of Dionysus who was the patron, the God, of the theater. And then we have to use another language altogether for doing psychology. We have to imagine it as a realm of Dionysian life. Of life force, of passion, of tragedy and comedy and not a clarification that you would get from an Apollonic or an Athenian or another perspective of what goes on. Also, it seems to me that Dionysus has tried to get into therapy for a long, long time as an unwanted visitor.

SS: I hear Jung's applied for training a few times as well.

JH: I don't know, that training would be interesting. But it implies break-ins of the unwanted forces of nature, passion, revelry, violence, and so on, that are supposed to be kept out of the *temenos* in a way—or at least brought in and held within the vessel—this would be the reappearance of the Dionysian, which is there authentically in the psychodramatics of engaging with the other persons. It's a theater.

SS: The term Jung explicitly uses is that this is his own mystery play. This is his *mysterium*.[34] And it's not yours. So that the engagement is with his own drama. He's struck by the words of the French novelist Léon Daudet who wrote a work on the "Interior Drama."[35] Jung is taken by this expression. His thought develops in this work as an interplay between characters. They stage positions and also are tremendously cultural and historical. So in his encounter with the good anchorite Ammonius, who I got to know quite well in working on this text, he is then retracing the shift from, or the coming together of, Greek philosophy and Christianity: his meditation on the significance of the Logos, the Word.[36]

JH: But in dramatic form.

SS: In dramatic form, and hence it's set in a Libyan desert, where he meets this anchorite. His fantasy takes him back. He's on set. He's on location where this took place. But he's not writing a text, he's actually encountering a figure. And they're having a theological debate.

JH: Well, that's a play. That's a drama. By the way, did you work, speaking of the anchorite in the desert, did you do most of your work in daytime, in the morning, fresh, or did you work at night, late? Just a personal question.

SS: At all hours.

JH: All hours.

SS: There's a French poet, Saint-Pol-Roux, who fixed on his door the statement when he went to sleep, "Don't disturb. The poet is working."

JH: So it was always going on. Well, thinking about the drama . . . you know, once you think of things in terms of drama, the whole work of actually engaging with your life is simply not just suffering and affliction but its backdrop is tragedy, and the whole daily world you're in, its backdrop is comedy. And that gives it such another vision to the tediousness of psychotherapeutic complaint.

SS: This is a *Commedia* in the truest sense of the word. A *Commedia* that encompasses tragedy and comedy.

JH: The whole range. Exactly.

SS: Jung says toward the beginning that the supreme meaning is also laughter. It's also the absurd.[37] That's in there too. It's not excluded. So it's not a ponderous tome. It's also a very funny work in places.

JH: This might be a good place for us to stop—this funny work, this comedy, this theater. What do you think?

II

Connecticut

SECOND CONVERSATION

JH: Psychology after the *Red Book*, that's our theme. We're going to assume of course there is a psychology, that there is such a thing and so on, but we don't know what the *Red Book* has already done to what we call psychology. How do you see that?

SS: We have now a peculiar opportunity for something to begin again because the foundational text was simply not available. It is now, and one can potentially reboot after a hundred years.

JH: And if it's a foundational text, then we have to in a sense put a bracket around what has been called psychology.

SS: So one sees the contingency of what has ensued over the last century.

JH: Well, there's the *Red Book*, but Jung's experience in the *Red Book* is about the psyche from the inside, *it* presents *itself* through *his* visions, *his* writing, *his* image, the depictions, and that we haven't really had previously. We've had visions of saints, we've had other kinds of interior experiences, but it's all been objectified in a strange way, differently objectified. Jung turned into a second language: that is measurement, report, and so on, but this is different, and that makes it much more immediate, in other words it's almost as if we're dealing with the psyche as it shows itself.

SS: One way I formulated it was that you have Swedenborg going into this visionary realm to create revelation, Blake doing so to create art, and Jung to create psychology, which is a different enterprise and purpose.

JH: If psychology after the *Red Book* is our theme, what is that psychology going to be? What is the *Red Book* telling us about the psyche? What came to Jung in this book?

SS: What he grapples with is the weight of human history and ancestry. He realizes that he can't move forward without going back, without understanding the implications that the past weighs on him, and this is not purely in a personal sense, which has been the main preoccupation in psychology, but with history as such, and in particular with taking up unfinished business, taking up unanswered questions.

JH: It's the history of the soul, so the history of psychology really means the history of the soul, and if psychology is to move it has to *speak* to the soul and it has to speak *about* the soul. That would be the objectification, but it has to speak *to* it, and that's what he finds a way to do, but we'll come back to that, as that's the crucial thing about psychological language, that psychology after the *Red Book* has to find another language, and we've got to talk about that. But this weight of human history is such a weight, maybe that's why the book weighs so much, and why it's such a big book. It *has* to be a big book. You know, there's a sentence from Hans-Georg Gadamer, one of the great minds of our time, who lived to be about one hundred himself, and he gave a talk in Naples at the philosophic institute, and he says in there something I wrote down: "A great mystery lies in the repetition and continuity of the renewal of that which is past. Culture perpetuates itself in memory and the big job is the reawakening of memory." Now isn't that what the *Red Book* does?

SS: It does, and it takes off from the fact that Jung had already completed a big book, *Transformations and Symbols of the Libido*, which he realized was insufficient. He'd already written a vast study of human history, of comparative mythology, the history of religions, and in fact he'd explained it all away—all of these myths, all of these figures—as symbols of libido, but in a certain sense they bit back. It was his own rationalistic explanation that was insufficient.

JH: And he felt that?

SS: Yes.

JH: So the break that everybody likes to talk about, the break with Freud, was over that book, and it was not only that Freud didn't accept that book but Jung himself didn't fully accept that book.

SS: He didn't accept it for radically different reasons. He hadn't done justice to the material, and he begins that book by contrasting two forms of thinking, rational directed thinking and undirected fantasy thinking, so while he is looking to study the interplay of these two and the persistence and perseverance and significance of fantasy thinking today, the book is written from the standpoint of direct thinking. It's a rational text on fantasy thinking.

JH: It's packed with fantasy figures and mythological figures and textual figures.

SS: And they're explained away. What Jung then finds at the same time is that a double movement is taking place. While he's working on this, the figures are working on him. They are stimulating his own fantasy.

JH: That's between 1911 and 1912–13.

SS: So he's finished the book but the material hasn't finished with him and he has to reapproach it from a different angle, which is the question of to what extent is this form of thinking still active and alive in himself?

JH: And that's where the *Red Book* begins, with the sense that he's lost his soul. So part of his loss of soul, or his sense of loss of soul, was, look, I've discovered how the psyche works but somehow it hasn't awakened my own soul, it hasn't solved *my* problem.

SS: Well he's done it in a supposedly objective manner. He's left himself out of the equation.

JH: Psychology after the *Red Book* means your own equation has to be in it.

SS: Yes. That's absolutely essential.

JH: But your own equation, meaning the personal, *my* soul, that sense of *my* soul, is not what psychology has said was the personal. Psychology says the personal is my history, my parents, my childhood, the trauma, my life, my wounds, my aspirations, all of that, that's *me*, that's my soul, the deepest feelings and loves and pains that I carry. Jung is saying the deeper soul is not personal at all, in a very curious way. He's saying it's an objective soul that is the deepest personal. It's only Jung who writes the *Red Book*, but all that material in there doesn't have his parents, doesn't have his marriage, doesn't have his tribulations, the personal isn't there, but it is intensely and deeply personal. So the idea of the personal has to be rethought.

SS: He finds that his innermost, the most deeply subjective, is no longer subjective and that it opens out into something far larger, and that's what in a certain respect saves him. In the depths of his solitude, his isolation, in his confrontation with himself, he finds an opening. He finds that what animates his depths is the weight of human history, in the sense of the figures he encounters there, such as the mythic figures and biblical figures. His deepest conflicts are expressed in the form of the interplay between these images.

JH: His deepest conflicts are expressed in the interplay between the images? That's very profound. Because it's always imagined in usual psychology that the deepest conflicts are between my life, *me*, in some strange way, and various other figures, but to begin with there are conflicts within the figures, among the figures, there are tensions, let's put it that way, not conflicts, tensions, and announcements or revelations that reveal my psyche and yet are historical, objective, in that sense curiously impersonal, never happened to Jung, they're not part of his history in the personal sense. So that's a big change. I'm living what Auden said: "We are lived by powers we pretend to understand."[38] It's the powers who give us our deep personal life. The understanding that we use to understand all this usually in psychology is actually a pretension if we follow Auden—you pretend to understand, it's a *pre*tense.

SS: This is what Jung realizes, that what he had hitherto taken to be psychology had been an explaining away. He thought he'd encompassed the soul, but he'd turned the soul into a dead formula, and his attempted explanation had simply killed off the subject matter. The subject matter in this sense—it's quite specific—is fantasy. His own fantasy had dried up under the weight of the pretensions of explanation. The psychiatric and psychoanalytic—in the 1912 sense of rational explanation—had simply expired in that if you look at the formal explanation it's tracing back fantasy to personal determinants, to complexes.

JH: But then he says right after, later, when he validates the other kind of thinking, the dereistic, as it's called in the English translation, that is, "away from reality" or fantasy thinking, he validates that later in volume six, where he says this is the basic activity of psychic life, this fantasy making, and he uses the term "image," not from afterimage, something you've experienced or seen, but he says he takes it from poetic usage.[39] Now that's a huge step.

SS: That's one of the main results he arrives at after the *Red Book*.

JH: Well then I think psychology after the *Red Book* has to be based on the fantasy image. It has to use the language of the poetic, or the analogous, or the metaphoric, or anything that is not, so to speak, denotative.

SS: One finds within the work two levels of language. First is what one could describe as practice of the image. In the fantasies themselves, he tries to enter into the unfolding of dramatic sequences, he enters into the fantasy, he engages with the figures. This is the first level. The second level—I describe this as layer two—is in the level of lyrical elaboration that occurs from 1914 onward, when he realizes that his fantasies in part were prophetic. Within this he tries to understand the general significance of the image, but in the most striking passages, by allowing them to resonate, allowing them to unfold in a metaphorical manner, he encounters for instance the figure he calls "one of the lowly" and this leads him to meditate on his own lowliness, his own destitution, his own beggarliness, so that the figure then unfolds in a metaphorical dimension rather than being translated into a conceptual form. He tries to remain within the imagistic terrain of the fantasies.[40]

JH: Which is exactly what a poet does. A poet doesn't translate his poems into what they mean, he goes into the language and the description of the beggarly, and he'll find the beggarly analogous in different ways: a fallen leaf or a piece of turd or something, and by the time you've gone through the poem you have had the experience of that destitution. The difference between what the poet does and what Jung does is that the poet has certain rules that he or she must obey—even in free verse a certain poetic form will structure what's said. Jung doesn't have that. He uses other aesthetic means to present, for example, the drawings or figures or paintings, or possibly the calligraphy, but he has rules too. They're not the rules of psychology though, are they? As the poet has the rules of poetry. Poetics?

SS: He's inventing the rules as he goes along. He's trying to find his way, trying to find what is right and fitting expression and what form that should take. So it's a linguistic experiment to find right and fitting expression that is reflecting back on a series of fantasies a year later and thinking, pondering the significance of his engagement. This is the reflective dimension of retrospective engagement.

JH: But when a voice says to him "This is art" and he says "No, it's not art,"[41] although he's tempted, he's rejecting or he's realizing how close what he is doing is to what a musician or a composer must experience when a flood of music comes. He has to put it into a form, express it in the language of music. How do you express this in a language that's not art, not poetry, but in the language of psychology? Isn't that the reflection that he's trying for? Or maybe not even in the language of psychology. How do you find the language for what's happening?

SS: That's certainly there, but let's stick to this question of art for the moment. Jung himself maintains the nineteenth-century conception of art, so paradoxically when he says "This is not art" it is bringing him into the most radical proximity to the European avant-garde who are in the process of dismantling traditional conceptions of art. So in a way, without realizing it, he's throwing off an outmoded conception of art.

JH: That's interesting. He's throwing away, or out, an outmoded conception of art. So this is not art, meaning this is not *that kind* of art.

SS: Yes, this is not symbolism, or this is not art for art's sake, in terms of certain aesthetic currents in the late nineteenth century. This is not Flaubert, this is not Maupassant.

JH: That one I have to really think about. We've got to deal with that somehow. That sentence "This is not art." First of all the voice that says "This *is* art."

SS: Well, I take that to be the voice of one of his close associates at this time, Maria Moltzer, and if you look at her own understanding, she sees art as something ultimately religious, so that by saying it's art, the strength of the statement is saying this is no longer in some sense science. Look for instance at Kandinsky's text *Concerning the Spiritual in Art*. Art for Kandinsky is about spiritual renewal.[42] The painting of the nineteenth century was no longer fitting, no longer serving the purpose that art had. It was an attempt to completely reformulate art as something which could lead to spiritual awakening.

JH: And you think Maria Moltzer's vision of art was closer to that?

SS: Yes, closer to that.[43] But this is why the question was troubling Jung.

JH: Troubling Jung, troubling me too. I didn't know whether you said "Jung" or "you." It's troubling me because Jung's notion of art at that time as *I* see it were those images on the walls of his parents' house, which were just conventional, but you think Jung had a much deeper understanding of contemporary art at that time?

SS: I don't think he did, but I think that he did without realizing it, which is the more interesting aspect, so that if you take the situation in 1902, he goes to Paris, he goes to the Louvre, this is the type of work he's looking at, and he has some of the traditional paintings there copied. If you look at some of his own early paintings, they are influenced by German Romanticism and artists such as Böcklin. That's the type of conception of painting he has.

JH: So this is not that. That sentence is saying, "What I'm doing is not that." But he's also denying in a way what Maria Moltzer meant. This is a spiritual art.

SS: Yes, that's the other movement he wishes to avoid, which is, this is revelation, simply present the material as it is.

JH: So the great problem he has is what do I do, since he remains committed as a psychologist, or a psychiatrist, committed to the act of reflection upon what's happening, the act of understanding what's happening, that's the crucial thing. It's not the content only, it's how do I understand and express this content?

SS: That's what makes Jung *Jung*. That is what is most interesting about him. It's insufficient for him simply to present the elaboration of the material. He wants to understand the process: Why did I think this? How did I paint this? What is this all about? It's that reflective dimension.

JH: And also, why is this happening to me? To *me*? I think some of that has to do with this working through Christianity, which he felt was a crucial problem of his.

SS: Still on this question of art and the aesthetic dimension, I remember at one point in discussion with the editor Jim Mairs he was looking at the issue of whether there was an image that could go on the cover of the book and we were moving to the position that we should just have it as red. He had an issue persuading his marketing department that you have a book full of images with nothing on the cover. He said, I hate to say this but it's not as if any of the images themselves are in their own right beautiful images as such. This is not Picasso, this is not Klee, this is not Kandinsky, and yet they are tremendously forceful, particularly within the context of the work as a whole.

JH: They don't stand alone in that way.

SS: We understood that when we tried to take an image out and there was nothing that stood *pars pro toto*.

JH: That in a way is a confirmation of the sentence "No it's not art," in the sense of a piece.

SS: And it also began to give a sense of the question: Why on earth is he painting this in a book? Why has he taken this particular form as opposed to painting on canvas, which he could do and had done? The separate paintings that he did—which are all linked to the cosmology of this book—are striking.

JH: There's a tradition of paintings in books. Medieval manuscripts and lots of things. Paintings standing alone is one kind, and then there's painting in books, but he preferred it in the book, right? So it belongs as an integral part of the work, of the *Red Book*. So you and Mairs came to the agreement that there's no image to put on the cover.

SS: And thankfully the marketing department agreed, against its "better instincts."

JH: The collective convention is to have an image on a book but that's not the French notion of books, for example; in *Spring*, we don't put images any longer on books, we just have the title of the book. The calligraphy is important, the typeface, which is imagistic itself. There's something though that is nonetheless similar to what the artist goes through, which is that things happen and they become elaborated. It's as simple as possible, and through skill, through craft, through dedication, through intensity, elaboration happens. And that's what Jung did with the things that happened to him, and the process, the parallel process, makes what Jung is doing art. You devote yourself, and you're not surprised by that which comes to you, you give it its due. Poets wait for a line to come, from which they can go on working, or a little melody is picked up in a bird's song, or a striking image comes and sticks with you, that's the beginning. Jung in that sense is an artist when he's working, is he not?

SS: *Malgré lui*. Without fully realizing it, he's in the company of people who are revolting against a view of art that has become moribund. For instance the Dadaists didn't see themselves any longer as artists and understood the work they were doing as a revolt against the collapse and decay of Western civilization. They saw the images they produced in an ethical dimension.

JH: But they had a program. I don't think Jung has a program. He's dedicated to what appears but he doesn't have a program of revolt, or annunciation. He's not a herald, when he's recording what happens to him, he's a disciple of what's happening.

SS: He doesn't have a program but he has a concern with meaning, which becomes the overriding directing principle. So the question becomes one of how best to grasp the meaning of the event, of the experience, how best to express the significance. That's what I see as the element that divides him most sharply from the Dadaists, who in a certain sense were expelling meaning, semantics. One thinks of Hugo Ball's sound poems—if they slipped into signification they would not have worked.[44]

JH: I'm thinking about this relation of art and meaning. There are two aspects to it and you've touched them both. One is, what does this painting mean, or what does this work mean, and the other is what does it mean *about* me, *to* me, *for* me, what's *my* meaning in doing this? That's a different thing, isn't it?

SS: Jung becomes more interested in understanding the process, so what the images of the work depict are his own iconography. He meditates on these images to grasp the implications for himself. He sees them as ciphers, as symbols, and uses them as icons.

JH: So these are statements about his soul that he needs to get the meaning of.

SS: His soul's revelation to him.

JH: Therefore his approach, as I would see it, is different from the man who paints and the man who writes music who has to adjust when he reads the notes he's written. He has to adjust certain parts because they don't work, as he would say. That didn't work, that line needs to be changed, the harmony here where the bassoon comes in is off, and so on, things like that. That's not what Jung's concerned with, in other words, making the form that he's working on fulfill itself. He's got a different kind of reflection. He doesn't look at the painting and say, "I don't know if that works," "I think there's too much that," "I'd got to rub all that out" or "I've got to put something else in" or "Do it again" or "Try another sketch." That's not what Jung's reflection is. It's not artistic reflection, it's psychological reflection.

SS: Yes, yet at the same time, paradoxically, it's because he's not in a way concerned with his own aesthetic criteria, given that he has nineteenth-century aesthetic criteria. The odd juxtapositions are just far more close to artists who are deliberately trying to break down those conventions.

JH: So he is, *malgré lui*, in spite of himself, doing contemporary art.

SS: Yes, because he's saying, I'm not caring about convention. For other reasons. He's not directly engaged in a war against classicism, aestheticism, and so forth, this is not his concern.

JH : And it's not derivative in any way of what was going on, such as the Symbolists of the time. He's not derivative of that movement.

SS: No, and he also is clearly looking at the art or pictorial work of other cultures: the Aztec, the Maya, the Indian, the African, and so on. Without realizing it, he's doing exactly what Picasso, Braque, and Klee are doing. But they're looking at these materials for aesthetic inspiration. Jung is not looking at it for aesthetic inspiration. Yet he's probably closer to the intention in those works.

JH: Closer to the intention in those works in the sense of the expression of the psyche.

SS: Yes, in that these were not works that were, as art historians tell us, intended as artworks initially, they were ritual objects. Jung's actual work is closer to the spirit of some of these non-European arts.

JH: But the ultimate task that he has is understanding what he has produced.

SS: That's the overriding purpose. It's insufficient simply to articulate.

JH: Why then does he not understand better what was produced by Joyce and what was produced by Picasso later on?[45] I say later on because this is after he's done the *Red Book*. He would have the knowledge of that kind of work, this extraordinary eruption of what Joyce called Nighttown, for example, at the end of *Ulysses*, or Picasso's descent into the underworld as Jung called it. Why was he not sympathetic to what they did in light of what he had been through?

SS: They were like crazy brothers, they were doppelgängers—
"There, but for the grace of God, go I"—in that they indicate a
path not taken and hence the intense irritation that immediately
strikes one as quite bizarre in the context of Jung's other writings.

JH: That he wrote those two essays?

SS: Yes, in those two essays compared to his other writings.
These works are in a way too close for comfort as they approach a
similar terrain from a different vertex.

JH: Yes, that makes good sense. In other words, they're both
making a descent into the underworld, as he did, and have met
the figures, and he's recognizing the motifs he knew from his
own experience, but he still judges it as crazy, because they
don't come up with the meaning for them in it. Is that what his
judgment is? That they don't make a psychological move?

SS: Or that they appear to be simply exalting, reveling in it. The
nekyia becomes a bacchanal.

JH: And that offends him.

SS: It's almost as if—I don't know if this is too strong—it's
almost sacrilegious.

JH: Or unethical.

SS: It's a send-up of the holiest of mysteries.

JH: He doesn't respect in that sense the dedication of the artist to
the formulation as an act of devotion, as a religious act itself. That
Joyce's work and Picasso's work show the same religiosity in their

dedication and their sacrifice to the work, he doesn't recognize as what really goes on in the artist.

SS: I think he doesn't see that, and he also doesn't see the extent to which the form of presentation within Picasso and Joyce is sufficient unto itself. There's a *lumen natura*, to borrow one of the alchemical expressions Jung uses, already within the image. There's a translucency that doesn't require anything else.

JH: That's very nice. And the artist respects the *lumen natura* and wherever it goes.

SS: For Jung, it's insufficient.

JH: Now this leads to a real problem. What makes it sufficient for Jung is what you call meaning, which unfortunately has become translation, conceptualization, unfortunately, and that's where I think psychology, since that's our basic subject, has gone wrong. Let's say the *lumen natura*, the light of nature, which is in the phenomenon or the image, its expression, is enough. It requires for Jung one step farther, some formulation of understanding or meaning. The delicacy of that meaning must not collapse or descend or be perverted into the usual psychology.

SS: I think there are several important things to focus on here. First, Barbara Hannah reports that Jung stated his greatest torment was a torment of not understanding.[46] There is an overriding desire to comprehend, to understand. The second element there is within Jung's work on the images. There are two levels of comprehension. The first is within the *Red Book* itself, in this layer two, lyrical elaboration, and the second is within his attempt to translate this into conceptual language. Therein occurs a destruction. He's already comprehending the images in the second layer, he's already trying to look at the significance, but there is an evocation that takes place there that to my mind gets lost when he attempts to formulate it into a scientific psychology: and the word "science" is absolutely critical for him.

JH: So he can't get rid of his own first kind of thinking?

SS: No, he can't. He wrestles with the images, he wrestles with this language, which at the other side he himself is attracted to, and there's a tension.

JH: Exactly. It's a piece of him.

SS: There's a tremendous allure simply to give himself over to it.

JH: Which is exactly what Fechner did. When Fechner was about forty he went through a crisis of three years, he went blind and all that. William James writes about Fechner,[47] Jung writes about Fechner.[48] He's one of my heroes, he was this great scientistic psychologist.[49] He threw it all over and came out and said the night world is the real world and the day world is not the real world and everything was turned upside down and he lectured in another section of his university, out of science. Jung didn't do that, he kept both sides.

SS: And Fechner would have been in his view as something he did not want to do.

JH: That he did *not* want to do.

SS: To move from psychophysics to the soul life of plants. And he would have witnessed the ridicule in conventional psychological circles—James is clearly an exception—that Fechner's late works were met with. Particularly given the fact that Jung would have had the sensibility to have appreciated these works.

JH: This is the part of Jung that's afraid of, what he said, "going black" if he were to stay in Africa too long, the fear of giving in totally to what he called dereistic thinking, away from reality thinking, the second kind of thinking, personality number two in *Memories, Dreams, Reflections*.[50]

SS: It's a fear of going native and becoming a denizen of the underworld and not returning to the surface.

JH: Does he see that in Picasso and Joyce?

SS: I think he does. So that you have the epigram in the first section of *Psychology and Alchemy*: a citation from Virgil where he's saying in effect that it's not the descent that is difficult but returning to the upper air, that is the real task.[51] To simply remain down there would be a cop-out. But to try—and he states this on numerous occasions—to be able to communicate to the contemporary outlook, to be able to formulate for the contemporary world or to reformulate the contemporary worldview.

JH: It's a cop-out to stay down there.

SS: Hence Joyce and Picasso he sees as reveling in the Walpurgisnacht, the witches' sabbath, the carnival.

JH: What strikes me is the moment when we were at a seminar as students, somebody asked about something or other, and he took off like a madman against Albert Schweitzer. This is the first time I've got an insight into that. He was against Schweitzer then, and I always saw it then as a certain enmity, or envy. Schweitzer was the great hero, the white man's hero, doing so many good things for the Africans and so on and so forth. But now I see what it was. He accused Schweitzer in that diatribe, "it was a cop-out," was what he was saying. He copped out, he stayed in Africa where anybody can be a saint and do good work for people who are starving or help sick natives. But he wasn't coming back to the European realities, which were so horrible, really horrible during that period. That was his accusation, but now you've put it within a different context. You've put it within the basic context of the descent. You've got to return from the descent. So he was taking Africa partly symbolically or metaphorically there. Schweitzer stayed in Africa and avoided the real job, which was the return.

SS: You find the same sensibility, the same reaction, in his papers on yoga.[52] He's saying study it, but for God's sake don't do it. Hence his tirades against "decking out in false feathers," in the sense that the European should not simply take the easy route and meditate but should return to find an equivalent of European heritage, which is Christianity. Simply to enter into the flora and fauna of Eastern symbolism would again be a cop-out.

JH: Well, of course the critics of Jung called Jung a cop-out, that in his trip to India he turned away from the holy men of the East, and he couldn't really go with them into the full range of the spiritual. That's the critique.

SS: I think that if you look at his alchemy copy books,[53] which give some sense of his trip in India, he's looking at the symbolism. This is what's attracting him, and while he's not prostrating himself before the feet of a guru, he is seeking and speaking to priests, inquiring as to the meaning of symbolism.

JH: And when he asks those questions, also in the American West, he's always amazed that they don't have any idea what these things mean, because they're not interested in them!

SS: And yet he admires it because they have something that he sees the West has lost, which is this imminent dwelling within the cosmos. He longs for this, but he himself is the most furthest removed from it, precisely because of his quest for meaning and understanding.

JH: Does he come to terms with the figure in himself that requests meaning? Does he come to terms, because that would be the task, the way I understand archetypal psychology, that you must always understand who is asking the question. The task is not to get the answer, the answer is who is dominating my mind, so that that's my basic question, who is determining my point of view. It's like a deconstructive "I." You don't just want to get an answer. The real answer is "Why is that my question?" Does he ask that question? Does he ask, Why is meaning so bloody important? Why must I understand?

SS: I think you have tensions in Jung. On the one hand there's the figure that builds the tower in Bollingen, that makes the stone he puts these cryptic citations on, that paints his murals in the tower in the room he calls the chapel and is happy to dwell within his own cosmology, remote from others, simply to dwell with his own figures. And yet on the other hand, around the same time, say the 1950s, there is Jung the figure who's bemoaning the fact that there's no one in the West who can understand him, who's making an effort to reach the populace. He is not content with finding a solution for himself but wants to provide a means of understanding that would be of therapeutic benefit for others.

THIRD CONVERSATION

SS: Jung spent sixteen years of work largely transcribing the typed manuscript into the calligraphic volume and adding the paintings. This was something done for others as well as for himself.

JH: So it was clearly not self-indulgent, in the sense that he was imagining that artwork has a basic problem in it, and that in some ways both Joyce and Picasso, who published and exhibited their work, nonetheless indulged in that aspect of their art. This was exaggerated enormously in some artists and less so in others.

SS: "Doing it" is insufficient. He's conflicted about the effects that making his work public at certain junctures will have. He's conflicted precisely because of the issue of sacrificing where he's got to in terms of public standing, his persona. Will he himself be seen as an artist? Will anyone then take his psychology seriously qua universal science? Yet at the same time he's not leaving it, and I think that he becomes, I suppose, ultimately resolved for the work being made posthumously available.

JH: It had to be published to fulfill his notion that otherwise it's self-indulgent, it's only *his* private tower.

SS: He states repeatedly that, central to his involvement and engagement with the material, he felt something in it concerned others, that this was not purely personal. As he states, recorded in *Memories*, he then belonged to generality.[54] Something had taken place in him, he had witnessed something.

JH: It's not just your own personal opinion, it's something in the work. It's *lumen naturalis*, the inner light of the image, and maybe the inner light of the image asks to be seen by the world. Maybe revelation or enunciation isn't something a person decides about. It comes with that strength within it, what the French call an *idée force*, there's a force in the idea, and that needs to come into the world some way or another.[55] Now it could come into the world as prophecy, but we'll talk about that another time. For Jung it's a moral matter, that it not be self-indulgent, that the meaning is not completed unless the meaning for others is involved. It's not just meaning for him. Am I right about that?

SS: And that what he underwent had consequences for others. This is what he realizes at several levels. He finds he's fallen into a stream of images. What then is played out within that stream of images is the conflict between the ancient and the modern, between the pagan and the Christian.

JH: Between the orthodox or conventional Christian and the heretical Christian.

SS: He never doubts that this is of wider relevance. The question is how to return this to the upper air and not be derided, to take the lines from Nietzsche's *Dithyrambs of Dionysus*: "Only a fool, only a poet," to not be laughed at.[56]

JH: Which is one of the ways it has been or would be taken anyway, by those who have no understanding of the material as such. I'm not worried about them particularly. I mention it in passing. But the publication of the book is a consequence of the process of his thinking about art, and about the self-indulgence of only doing your thing, whether your thing is going to Africa, your thing is yoga, your thing is painting or writing music, only doing your thing, a dedicated doing of your thing, is still not enough. There is something more required. And there is a theory of art that says—I'm thinking of Klaus Ottmann—that paintings are fulfilled only when they are viewed. It's the viewer who fulfils the work.[57]

SS: Jung has a conception that is very strong, that as an individual you have a responsibility to society that you must fulfill.

JH: And you can't split that off by fulfilling it as a doctor, or as a psychiatrist, or as a father of the family, which is what he did, but that isn't the whole game. The art has to be connected to society.

SS: Also there's a paper in 1916 where he says that if you remove yourself from society, you have to return with an equivalent in the form of a work.[58]

JH: That's a very important observation.

SS: You have to bring something back, that's the tax for going off.

JH: Bring something back, to the world, to society. Well then the publication of the book becomes absolutely essential to the fulfillment of the book.

SS: And also to his work, to his whole work. I don't think it's going too far to state that in a certain sense what he did post-1930 in his work is in part a preparation for the publication of this work. What he's presenting in his alchemical opus is the contextualization. What he's presenting in the form of the cross-cultural study of the process of individuation is the wider setting for this work—for the *Red Book*—in the sense that what he does in his engagement with Christian theology is to show that this image he has, this theophany of God as the son of the earth, as the son of the frogs, is no mere idiosyncratic raving of a lunatic but bespeaks the transformation that is happening in contemporary culture, of the transformation of the Godhead that is taking place within the world. So the later work in a way is a setting—

JH —which gives the *Red Book* its context.

SS: And then you can likewise see how the later work comes about, you understand it in historical context. You can see the making of his psychology. But at this point, in a way the later work, this is no mere prestage that is discarded in the way in which, for instance, Freud's letters to Fliess are, in the sense you can see what then emerges out of it but you receive no new content from it, it gives you no radically new conception of Freud's activity.[59] You see the prestages. That's a conventional sense of a certain type of precursor or prototype. No, this is really something quite radical, which reformulates how you understand this man's work. It shakes the whole thing up. And in a way it confirms certain aspects that you can see, and that readers with sensibility have been able to appreciate, aspects where the seams are exposed, places in the later publications where you automatically dip your foot into it, to change metaphor.

JH: No, it's important to understand that it's not a precursor, because one of the criticisms of the publication is, well, these were Jung's crazy scribblings, notebooks, diaries, half-formed thoughts, and that kind of stuff belongs in the drawer and doesn't belong out in the public, because what belongs in the public is the finished work, where he's been able to put his mind to it. These are early works that are not really important, not just early works but incomplete works. Now in fact this is an absolutely invalid criticism, because the work is highly articulated, highly mastered and fifteen years of it or more. So *that* criticism, that this shouldn't come out because it's just ordinary scribblings that anybody does in their notebooks, is not valid at all.

SS: One clear analogy that Jung himself has, which he refers to in a certain context, is the second part of *Faust*, which Goethe leaves in a drawer. Jung sees the second part of *Faust* as Goethe's masterwork but it's not published in his lifetime.

JH: That's the highest achievement, that's not early scribblings . . .

SS: Not early scribblings, and also it's something that Goethe spent a lifetime reflecting on, as Jung did on the *Red Book*. It's striking and moving to see that around 1958 Jung is conversing with Aniela Jaffé, and he says, you're right, the *Red Book* is not finished yet,[60] and he then, after an interruption of thirty years, goes back and tries to complete the transcription. It's moving to see that this is, was, his great unfinished task. There he is, picking up a transcription that was left off around 1928 or 1930 that itself is picking up fantasies from 1914. He tries to finish it and then leaves off, it's too much. Then he can't even summate his epilogue, even that becomes too much.

JH: It seems to my mind that's utterly appropriate. Anything he would have done would have narrowed what was—the idea of a summation.

SS: There's too much to say, it's beyond him. He would have to turn into his own biographer, which, as he wrote to many of his friends at that time, was a dreadful situation that he was finding forced upon him.

JH: Thinking of something else, though, that the justification for all the other works—I don't mean the studies of alchemy and mandalas and the *Tibetan Book of the Dead*, but the conceptual works—are part of his attempt to understand, rather than just to translate it into concept. At the same time that he does this he attempts to understand by means of usual psychological language, or his conceptual language: even anima and animus are concepts the way they've become. He has to again and again break into his descriptions by saying these are "only." He cuts them down as he puts them forward. He distrusts them. But still that's what we're left with. Now, you have said we shouldn't be left with that. But you admit that in Jung's own nature there's a terrific desire for a language, for expression, to find the language for what's happened. Maybe we have to rethink that question of the language, not the language that he's used—anima, animus, shadow, self, process of individuation—and discard *that* language, but not altogether a language that is already available in the arts, let's say, where they're wrestling with these problems all the time.

SS: Another term to introduce here is that of "myth." In his preface to *Symbols of Transformation*, Jung says that after writing the 1912 work *Symbols of Transformations of the Libido*, he then asks himself what was his myth? He had to get to know his own myth. Now, let's take it that in the course of his exploration he found his myth, that then is insufficient, so if the question in 1912 is "I needed to know what my myth was," by 1930 he'd found it. Now the question was how could he help others find their own myths. Simply to find one's own myth, simply to find one's own way in the world, to be able to find meaning in one's own existence, is insufficient, or it was insufficient for Jung. He had to find a way to enable other people to find their own myths.

JH: So that would be his myth?

SS: That then is a further aspect to it, or his myth in the form of his self-figuration as the shaman, the medicine man, of the West, which he articulated at several junctures.[61] His job is ferryman to the underworld and back, not simply to have just gone there and to stay there, which comes back to his issue of his criticism of Joyce and Picasso. They've taken the boat and just waved "bye-bye" to the day world.

JH: Except that both of them had a huge influence on people's lives and work. Joyce *changed* writing, Picasso *changed* painting. They may have said bye-bye but their dedication to their work nonetheless was an equivalent to direct responsibility to others.

SS: It definitely was, but Jung sees it as simply an invasion of the night world, simply letting it overcome the day world. In his own language, just giving oneself over to the spirit of the depths.

JH: With regard to Joyce, he saw evidence for that in Joyce's daughter, who was supposedly insane. Yes, who carried the burden that Joyce didn't carry. But there's something here that isn't quite clear yet. When he's looking for this myth, what's his myth, like in the *Red Book*, where's my soul, basic questions. Isn't the myth that he's looking for the fact that *myth* is what he's looking for, not *my* myth. You see, I think that has been a big problem, that each person reading Jung comes out and thinks, I've got to find my myth. What is my myth? What myth am I living? And it gets narrowed into some astrological declaration of whatever kind you are, or myth of the puer, myth of the hero, myth of the anima, myth of the unwanted daughter, I mean just ridiculous things. *Myth* is what he wanted. Joe Campbell would say *myth* is the hero, not the hero myth, but *myth* is the hero, myth is the thing that enlivens, myth is the actual psychic energy expressed in language and forms and figures.[62] Myth is the metaphor that translates libido into configurations. That's what he found. He found myth as basic.

SS: One critical aspect of that is the notion that to find one's own myth is inherently contradictory. I use the term, which I've mentioned, "personal cosmology." I use it deliberately because it's contradictory. How can a cosmology be personal? So he's not saying he had to find his own idiolect, which then could take one into a solipsism. The very notion to evoke the term *myth* implies something of generality. You can't have a myth if it's just yours. You're then talking about an idiolect. You're saying you've found something and it's your own story, but that's your own story, it's nothing more than that. That's insufficient for Jung. That's not what he's talking about. That would be in his criticism, for instance, his clarification of what he calls individuation. It's not simply about individuality, it's not idiosyncratic, following one's own journey, just for the hell of it, this is not what he's talking about.

JH: Yes, he's very strong on that.

SS: That's why the question then is still with him. Okay, he's done this, but the question of generalities is there.

JH: For others, for all, the universality of what he's dealing with.
    I'd like to return to the idea of return, the idea that Jung had expressed, that most important for Jung is not the self-indulgence

of the work, whether it's the *Red Book* or whether it's all the various things we've talked about, art or yoga or whatever, but the return to the world, to human value of the general. There's a responsibility to bring it into the life. Now it seems to me that this is where the trouble is, that Jung *did* find a way to bring it into life, which was his conceptual system. The self, individuation process, consciousness, the unconscious, the ego, then the archetypes of animus, anima, shadow, and so on. Now this language is one way of bringing it back into the world so that it can be shared by other people. But I think this way is inadequate. I think this is where Jung failed, if you will, a hard thing to say, but I think this is where it fails. I think there's another way, there are several other ways of bringing it back, one being what he actually did in practice, which was to teach people the method of active imagination. That was a way of bringing it back without that conceptual apparatus, which is unfortunately person-bound, individual-bound, and doesn't truly do the job of the return. This is the most important thing, as it has to do with psychology after the *Red Book*—another way of finding the return, of bringing this extraordinary experience of the depths of the psyche, and the weight of human history, back into human life, individual human life.

SS: My first thoughts on this is that there were intimates in Jung's circle, in the 1920s, with whom he shared this work, within his own practice. His whole endeavor was to enable individuals to find and articulate their own myth. It was often said at that time that you could understand Jungian psychology only through meeting Jung and this was something that concerned him, because he knew that there was a certain truth to it, that he hadn't put it in the books and you weren't going to be able to pick it up through the books. It was something that he could convey. So there's a sense that for those who had a personal encounter with him, they knew what he was on about, and they then knew how to read the published works, could distinguish the esoteric clues and see what was just the exoteric cover. It was at this one point where Cary Baynes talks about his books being written out of the head and not out of the heart, in the fire with which he spoke, for instance, at the Polzeath seminars.[63] Tina Keller, who worked with Jung during this period, said she found herself disappointed to read his later works.[64]

JH: Greatly disappointed to read his later works. But he taught her active imagination.

SS: But that fire wasn't there. So I think this was something he was aware of. The question was, how great was the cost. He's now in a position to begin to be able to look at the enterprise of translating his own experience and first articulation of them into a conceptual frame acceptable to a medico-scientific public.

JH: That's it. That was the idea of the return he had. Personality number two had to somehow be expressed through personality number one.

SS: The tragedy was that his work was never really accepted by the medico-scientific public, so was that effort worth it?

JH: Yes, was that effort worth it? I think at this point, because now we're in another time of history, and another time, what needs to be returned is not just what he experienced with these particular dialogues and the work of the *Red Book* but the weight of human history, which is the crucial thing, the dead. The dead have to come back. Do the dead, or the voices of the dead, come back through that conceptual structure? I don't think they do.

I don't think they come back through the amalgamation of the individuation process with developmental psychology, as it is expressed in so many of our colleagues' work. This amalgamation of personal history from childhood, parental family, combined with individuation as a journey through the opposites and so on. This language doesn't bear the weight of human history. It's *my* life, it's not human history. And it's the weight of human history, the voices of the dead, opening the mouth of the dead and hearing what they have to say, not just the deep repressed or the forgotten, it's the actual living presence of history in the soul, the past in the soul. We don't have a language for that in psychology. I think there *is* a language for that, I think Jung moved in that direction through anthropology and archaeology—which was his earliest interest, archaeology, that is, actually digging up the remnants of the past. But we *do* have a language that would begin to express it. We have it in the Greek plays, we have it in literature, we have it in works of art, we have it in the *Commedia* of human life. If that is studied rather than psychology studied, if philosophy is studied, the writings of the fathers of the church, the very things that Jung used, Neoplatonic philosophy, the things that Jung used in the language that he discussed with his figures, this would bring back, I think, some of this weight of history, and we'd have a different kind of imagination about what goes on in the psyche than the language that he used for his return.

SS: Well, before coming to the issue of history I want to say a little bit more about his conceptualism. There's a sense I get that he saw it as offering a safety rail for those who would be unable to encounter themselves without it. It had an apotropaic function, but one that nevertheless was of therapeutic benefit and utility to some people.

JH: A safety rail. It's curious, because he didn't have that safety rail himself, he didn't use those terms when he was engaging with the figures.

SS: Quite the opposite. So you get expressions like "This was the night on which all the dams broke,"[65] the face-to-face with the chaos of primal experience, primal as, in this case, *figural* experience.

JH: Figural experience. And taking everything that occurred, he engaged with everything literally, as it occurred.

SS: And his system had broken down.

JH: Yes, his conceptual system.

SS: It wasn't holding him.

JH: He didn't try, in the midst of it all, to diagnose the figures, or himself, or what he was going through in psychiatric language.

SS: Or even to turn back his figures into his own conceptual system.

JH: He didn't call them complexes of himself, even though he'd used the word "complex" for ten or fifteen years previously.

SS: Yes, he doesn't do this. This was a master hermeneut—he could have. He didn't do so because it was the wrong thing to do.

JH: Still he thought that, for the people he was working with, they needed that.

SS: They needed something. It had a therapeutic function, and he felt able to convey *something*.

JH: This is the tack that has been followed by the school of Jung since. We need this whole conceptual structure in order to take hold of experiences that are too explosive for the average person. I remember Barbara Hannah, you mentioned her, giving a course on active imagination at the Jung Institute years ago when I was there, saying it was almost a taboo, that you couldn't do active imagination unless you had a whole series of preliminary structures that could contain it and hold it. Then the London school would talk about how you can't do this unless you have a strong ego, that the first work is building the ego, freeing the ego from the parental inhibitions and restrictions et cetera. As if this was viewed from the point of view of the conceptual system, whereas within the experience Jung taught the method of engagement without that safety rail. I know I did it when I first began analysis in Zurich years ago. That was my analysis for years and I began absolutely naive, talking and just going down and discovering, not because I'd read Jung about how to do it. It wasn't a fear of these figures that were beginning to appear, and I didn't know what to do with them, and I sat at my table and closed my eyes and engaged with the first one that came. It's possible to do this, you feel very strange, because we're estranged from that world, but once you've done it, once the initiation has taken place, you don't need to come back every night and say I've engaged with the shadow and the shadow is black and violent, or the shadow is red and violent, and he's after this, or the anima is this or that. You don't need any of that. You're learning as you go, through the language that they teach you. So I wonder about this fear which was the word in Zurich in the 1950s when I was there, of "latent psychosis," that was the word. There was always a latent psychosis possible, and therefore you had to have all these rails.

Where did that all come from? Do you think that came from the group Jung had around him? He did go through what many have written about as a psychotic episode. How do you deal with all that?

SS: I don't see him, either within his own terms or within the psychiatric terms of the time, or today, as being in the least bit psychotic, or unhinged, or at any point on the verge of tipping over. In some sense, the fear of losing one's mind is a mark of one's sanity.

JH: Exactly.

SS: In my classes on history of psychiatry I begin each year by asking if there is anyone present who has not at some point in their life thought they might be on the verge of losing their mind. Some years no one puts up their hand, some years one, and that's usually the person you have to worry about! So that's not to say he's not encountering extremes and depths of his experience, or that he's not unaware it could have turned out differently—he *is* aware of this—but there's never a point, that I've seen, where what he's undergoing with his active imagination is bleeding over into his professional life, into his family life. I've spoken to family members about this issue and there was never any sign—

JH: He showed up for his meals.

SS: Yes, he played with his children.

JH: He kept his appointment book.

SS: He did his military service.

JH: And he wrote papers. He did his duties with the professional societies.

SS: And he could even write papers in a dull language that was not in the least bit florid! So the boundaries were always intact. It was controlled, yet clearly spontaneous things were happening, and he was aware that with other individuals in other circumstances it could have led to a different outcome.

JH: That's what he thought. Now we have to accept that judgment.

SS: It's also clear that with regard to the many individuals who came to see Jung in the 1920s and '30s, he had, you could say, a rich array of some of the most eccentric and neurotic people in Europe and the United States beating their way to his door, so you might say that he had people who were rather unhinged—

JH: And he was rather alone with his practice then.

SS: He's practicing in his house in Seestrasse. They were taking the train out to Küsnacht, many of these people were foreigners coming to Zurich, not knowing anyone there.

JH: Very isolated, cut off from their worlds.

SS: Yes, I remember Mrs. Hoerni, his daughter, telling me that he would sometimes ask his wife, Emma Jung, to go and look in on someone, to take tea with them, because they were just alone in Zurich. That's how Emma Jung began practicing herself, she got drawn in. It's as if he was designating someone almost as a social worker to look in on them.

JH: And that's why he started the club in 1916.

SS: Precisely for the same reason.

JH: So that these people would have a world of some sort. Some kind of reality.

SS: Someone they could talk to.

JH: So the rail that he was advising was *faute de mieux*, because there wasn't the rituals of daily life for these people, which held him. He was served not by duty and work, it was daily life as ritual, showing up on time, doing what was to be done. This was a way of *keeping* him that these people didn't have. That's what you're suggesting?

SS: He states explicitly that his family was a joy to him and convinced him of his own reality. He could shut the door to his study.

JH: But you see the inheritance of this is that sixty years later or seventy, eighty years later there's a world that follows this guide rail and is afraid, and it has put the weight of human history, all that incredible material, back down into the depths of the psyche. And it spends its time with the guard rail.

SS: Well, I think it's even worse than that. They've mistaken the guard rail for the essence.

JH: Exactly.

SS: So for instance if you take the collective unconscious as Jung's myth, as some have, then you think the conceptual system is the essence of his work, rather than his own personal cosmology. That is what I see as his myth, *not* the conceptual system. Everything gets turned topsy-turvy.

JH: That *has* taken place, and it's what I've been struggling with for fifty years. None of that feels like the palpable psyche to me. I'm aware of certain experiences I have that I would call anima possession, or I would feel infatuated and caught by the archetype of the anima, but I could just as well speak about Aphrodite, or about Venus, and I would be in a much closer relationship with that than if using the word "anima" as a complex or as an archetypal generality.

SS: I'm reminded of a story John Phillips once told me, how in the 1950s at the Jung Institute he went to Jung one day and said, Professor Jung, I've something that's been troubling me that I have to confess. I simply don't agree and don't believe in your theory of the anima. And Jung looked at him and winked and said, "I won't tell anybody." As if to say your secret's safe with me! I don't mind! But the curatorium would!

JH: Now, what I'd like to do in the last little bit of my life is promote another way, or another language, for the weight of human history, that psychology would emerge from the weight of human history by dealing with the same kinds of problems: possession, obsession, phobia, the languages of psychiatry and diagnosis, in terms of the world's arts and literature. You read Dostoyevsky, you read Tolstoy, you read Tennessee Williams, you read whatever you want to read, you read the Greeks, you read literature, drama, theater, plays, and you see the human comedy, the human tragedy presented to you in specific characters with whom you can identify, with whom you can feel the same things going on in them that are going on in me.

Your disturbance is given a remarkable background rather than a diagnostic background. The study in the work, the study of psychopathology, the study of therapy would be based in the depths, the weight, meaning the golden weight as well, of human history, it would be completely different. You'd still be able to use all your diagnostic terms but you'd be able to see obsessions, you'd be able to see them in terms of figures that help you carry your personal load of this weight, because you can't carry these things alone. You do need something to help you carry them, and the concepts help you carry them. But they don't feed you. The figures can feed you in the same way as the figures fed Jung through his dialogues with them. Personifications can be nourishing.

SS: It strikes me that what you're indicating or questioning is the role of what one can call psychological conceptualism. From a historical angle, I see psychological conceptualism as fueled by psychology's will to science, the notion that, from the end of the nineteenth century onward, psychology would be the science of sciences and it would provide the key that would explain the doer of science. That psychological language henceforth would be the equivalent of the periodic table. Psychological concepts would have that capacity and power to unlock, to interpret, all other languages, and it would replace precisely the weight of human history that you've evoked—it would replace literature, it would replace theology, with something that would lead to the equivalent of a calculus of probabilities.

JH: And it would be universal.

SS: Yes. Now in that regard, and also in that psychological conceptualism is privileged over all languages, you see that project still there in *Psychological Types*, where Jung is on the one hand drawn through this immense survey of historical literature that he's gripped by, but the whole time he is also saying what they are about. What is really at play here is the interplay between the functions.

JH: And introversion and extraversion.

SS: Yes. In my view, I think that that project, the will to science, didn't work in psychology and I think Jung himself was at times aware of this. What that then leaves one with, again from the historical angle, is to say, look, if psychology didn't work in the forming of the master discourse that explained all the others, then what did it actually do? In my view it then formed a language that was alongside the other—shall we call them folk psychologies, the nonprofessional forms of understanding that people use, for example, the psychology implicit in literature.

JH: And in fairy tales, for example. Folk psychology.

SS: It was simply one folk psychology among others but not a master key.

JH: With the validation that it was pseudoscientific. That gave it a certain aura.

SS: But at the same time you can also ask, What happens? Is psychology then a pure failure? I would say no. It is itself a valid folk psychology. What interests me is that it is a type of drift of language. For instance, people still talk of magnetic or mesmeric personalities, without believing in Mesmer's animal magnetism, or you speak of Freudian slips, without believing in Freud's libido theory or theory of repression.

JH: I see.

SS: To me, part of the beauty of language is it metaphorizes conceptual language. Conceptual language is, despite itself, figurative. It is a language of the articulation of experience, even though it tries and claims to be something else. It may be an impoverished figurative language but it still functions as such.

JH: Well, you're doing a lot for it. And I think only little bits of it work that way. If you look at dictionaries of psychology, such as James Dreaver's dictionary,[66] they're just packed with an unbelievable number of pseudoscientific terms.

SS: But the terms become taken on by people and they become, to adopt a phrase of the medical anthropologist Arthur Kleinman, illness narratives.[67] They become narratives in which they reform their lives.

JH: That's the DSM?

SS: Yes. Regardless of whatever validity they have, viewed from their initial scientific intent—

JH: And their denotative definition.

SS: —they become taken up by subjects. The question then shifts from a realism to whether there is or is not an Oedipus complex or an unconscious. That becomes too simplistic to take at a realist level. Well, there are people who have an Oedipus complex in their own terms. There are people who have an unconscious, in their own terms, and there are billions that don't.[68] What I see as important is to take away the universalism of one conceptual system and allow the other the right to describe its own experience in its own terms.

JH: It becomes, as you say, a folk psychology. So this is the language that they use, and it's put on the self-help shelves and you learn a set of terms that help you invent yourself, according to this language, or to frame yourself.

FOURTH CONVERSATION

JH: The *Red Book* depicts Jung's recovery of his soul. But by moving it to anima, which he does later, it becomes like a complex that you can deal with, and you lose some of that personification and what you call the fire.

SS: The term "anima" for Jung then is a makeshift, it's a sign. He is aware of what he's trying to evoke.

JH: Yes, no question.

SS: So when he speaks of it one gets the sense of the figural ground, the emotional ground behind it. It's not purely a concept for him. But with others, who took on these terms without that grounding, it became just conceptual coinage.

JH: It became a complex that hits you and then you have to deal with this complex, integrate it or something.

SS: What is it that from your perspective today strikes you about this book?

JH: The book somehow validated what I felt I was doing all these years without knowing it. I mean, my therapy of myself and my therapy with others, whenever possible, focused on active imagination, dialogues, encounters with figures, and teaching and learning how to deal with figures. So personification seemed to me absolutely the essential activity of the psyche, just as Jung says, or shows, in the *Red Book*.

What else? He says psyche is image or image is psyche—I never remember which is which, which noun comes first—and I've used that all along.[69] He says somewhere "stick to the image."[70] He says "dream the myth onward."[71] These are all keys to how to do psychology and how to do therapy. He doesn't use abstractions in the *Red Book*. I've tried to get rid of a lot of abstractions, such as the unconscious, or the ego, or the ego-self axis—even the word "self"—and to restore the weight of human history, meaning mythology, Greek mythology in particular, but also biblical figures or mythical fairy tale figures. I used the same kind of texts that Jung refers to, not so much gnostic but ancient philosophy. So all of the things that I was doing, and trying to write about, were all there in what Jung was doing in the *Red Book*. I was engaged with Christianity all along and said that both Freud and Jung had to come to terms with the deep unconscious, which was the weight of Christian history, or the psyche. In the *Dream and the Underworld* I have a chapter about that,[72] and in *Inter Views*[73] I have a chapter about that, and all through *Re-Visioning Psychology* I'm trying to work through the Christian prejudices. It seemed to me that without knowing it I was doing a parallel work in my own restricted and limited way to what Jung was dealing with in the *Red Book*.

SS: So that was the legacy you took up and without knowing that that was the case?

JH: But I didn't know that was the legacy. I didn't know it was so overt in the *Red Book*.

SS: Or necessarily that the questions you took as your own were questions that Jung left off.

JH: Exactly. And I found myself criticizing some of Jung's basic language, particularly his theory of opposites, presenting contrasts constantly in terms of opposites, and I found that that was an unnecessary mode of differentiation, a rhetorical mode. It's necessary for rhetorics to make a sharp contrast but it's not to be taken literally. I don't want to elaborate all that, it's a big thing to elaborate, but I've taken that position for years.

There's more, there's much more. It has to do with the reality of the image. When we talk about psyche we have to see what is presented phenomologically, or phenomenally, the images themselves, and they have everything in them that you need. And we're not concerned so much with the process of individuation, which is a developmental fantasy, but rather each thing presents itself as it presents itself, and it has all that you need already in it if you stick with it and work it and expand it. It's a metaphorical language. Also the psyche speaks in metaphors, in analogies, in images, that's its primary language, so why talk differently? We must write in a way that evokes the poetic basis of mind with a rhetoric that does not disabuse the psyche of its natural way of talking, and that requires a sensitivity to the words so that they *imply*, they *suggest*, it's a sensitivity to the language. That's a direct result of thinking nonconceptually.

SS: There's a striking episode in the work where the serpent soul speaks to Jung's "I," saying, "I give you payment in images."[74]

JH: Payment? Meaning riches?

SS: Riches. My gift is in the form of images. If you look at Jung's practice of the image, he often asks his soul or Philemon to explain to him what's happening, and even the attempt of explanation is contained within the image itself.

JH: The images explain themselves.

SS: He's asking one character to explain what the other character has said. The images are instructing him. He's allowing that to take place, indeed that's something that is marked right throughout the work. The figures make shocking statements, and he allows that to transform—

JH: He's being pulverized again and again by these figures. He doesn't like his own "I." The "I" in the dialogues he would like to disassociate himself from.

SS: The "I" is actually one of the most interesting figures, in terms of what befalls the "I" and what the "I" has to suffer and undergo and the transformations of the "I," but it's accomplished through allowing it to be subordinated to the other figures.

JH: It's very interesting. Back in the 1960s, I think, I gave a talk at Goldsmiths College, those art students in London, and I came up with this idea of the imaginal ego, the idea that we needed another ego, who was at home in the dream world, who spoke to the figures as one of them or something like that.[75] This is exactly what the *Red Book* confirms. I didn't do anything further with that, it was a little paper printed in there somewhere or other, but the idea is exactly that. The ego itself is just one of these figures, the so-called "I," and it's very uncomfortable in the underworld.

SS: In working on this text it took me quite a while to realize this, so initially I had it in terms of Jung talking to a character, and then I understood it's not Jung.

JH: Exactly, it's not Jung. It's part of the drama.

HILLMAN AND SHAMDASANI

SS: It's Jung's "I." Which is one character among others. In a sense it's all Jung.

JH: It's all Jung, but none of it's Jung.

SS: He is no more his "I" than he is his soul. And then the text opens up, radically.

JH: And if you think of this therapeutically, then the person opens up to realize that I, this "me" who I walk around with all the time, is actually a composite of a lot of people living in the same house. So who's talking now? Even as I sit here? Who's talking now? When you asked, it's very hard for me to put myself into the " me" sitting here, what I was thinking at another time, to explain something. It's very difficult, I can't do it easily. I much prefer not giving an account or a defense or an explanation or a promotion, or anything like that, as we have our dialogue. So it's almost as if we are part of an active imagination ourselves. Because the question of what it is about my work that connects with the *Red Book* puts me into a position of abstraction, and I'm uncomfortable. I can't say what I do, or what I did, it's very awkward. Yet I can do it.

And now this book is so crucial because it opens the door or the mouths of the dead. Jung calls attention to the one deep, missing part of our culture, which is the realm of the dead. The realm not just of your personal ancestors but the realm of the dead, the weight of human history, and what is the *real* repressed, and that is like a great monster eating us from within and from below and sapping our strength as a culture. It's all that's forgotten, and not just forgotten in the past, but that we're living in a world which is alive with the dead, they're around us, they're with us, they *are* us. The figures, the memories, the ghosts, it's all there, and as you get older your borders dissolve, and you realize I am among them, only it has that phrase living and partly living. You're living and partly dead, not dying but partly dead. As Higuchi, my friend from Japan, says, we are already in the afterlife. The afterlife is all around us. That book confirms the strength, reality— everything—of this afterlife which was recognized in Rome, which was recognized in Greece, which was recognized by the desert saints, which was recognized always, everything was talking to them. We have nobody to talk with. We are desperate and desolate, the ordinary individual. So that when one voice comes along and says one thing you think you're going crazy. This is how arid our desert is. So the book affirms what the collective, the world we live in, needs most of all things: remembrance of the smallness of your human personality in a world filled with figures.

SS: You could call it Jung's "Book of the Dead," in many respects.

JH: Yes, Jung's "Book of the Dead," excellent, a book in the *Bardo Thodol*.

SS: A *modern* "Book of the Dead." It's not a literal instruction to someone departing from life as the *Tibetan Book of the Dead* or the *Egyptian Book of the Dead*, but it's about imminence, it's about how "in the midst of life we are in death."

JH: The book is tremendously alive. There's tremendous violence in the book, and dispute and surprise and extraordinary figures from frogs to everything possible, plus the illustrations. We use the word "dead" to mean inanimate, cold, which is not the case.

SS: In this regard it's the most significant aspect of it, because he's saying that, as it were, the dead are alive, the dead are animated, and in a certain sense the living are dead, so that there are passages where he says that what is required is to be alone with one's dead and to recognize them, that is the work one has to take on. In his sense, he sees it as the redemption of the dead. This is a critical aspect of the myth that he articulates.

JH: Part of the work, the present work, is opening the mouth of the dead.

SS: What we see as our task, what we see in an individualistic manner, as our endeavors or our activities, is not such.

JH: So our task is nothing to do with getting better, and the path of individuation and so on and so forth. The task is living with the dead.

SS: What we take to be our individuation, in a personalistic sense, or our quest, or however one frames it, is not such. It is taking up the unredeemed dead, or taking up the tasks left by the dead, or the individuation of the dead.

JH: What they left us. What we have been bequeathed.

SS: And that's what we're left to work with. So that critically reframes it. What we take to be most particular in individuals is not such.

JH: The first thing that we have to do, the way of doing this, is opening all kinds of barriers, opening all kinds of walls that have been constructed, so that we're completely permeable, and that means allowing all kinds of whacky thoughts and dreams and fears, all sorts of things, to pass through.

SS: And it also goes back to what you were saying about the weight of history, in that a present is then animated by the past.

JH: We have to use a much richer language. He did. He used a rich language. He used the language of the figures of the dead actually: Philemon, Salomé, and so on. These come from a tradition. He didn't invent . . . well I don't know. Did he invent any names?

SS: He invents, for instance, the name of Atmavictu. But he invents him in a way that sounds as if he belongs in a lexicon of mythology![76]

JH: But besides that, whether he called him that, or whether that man, that figure came with that name, it's beside the point. The thing is that we would have to pick up historical background. Now I *did* do that, I was really sort of forced to find patterns. For example, with the *Dream and the Underworld*, I wanted to study the underworld, where dreams have their home and where they come from. We first have to look there, if we want to understand something about dreams. It seems to me that is what would have to be part of the language of a post–*Red Book* psychology, and it would have to incorporate the prescientific language. Prescientific in the sense that the scientific language objectified and therefore acted apotropaically against the other world.

SS: It never worked anyway, as we were discussing earlier. It itself got employed and used as a folk psychology. In my own endeavor, in working on Jung at a certain point of time, and this would have been around the time I first met you, I found that I fell out of psychology into history, and psychology seemed at that point just a chaos of conflicting opinions.

JH: That's so interesting. You see, I never did. I never really left psychology. And I still haven't. That's why I'm sort of tortured by it. But I remember the second or third *Eranos* paper I gave was called "The Language of Psychology and the Speech of the Soul,"[77] and I wanted to show this tremendous contrast between the language of psychopathology, with the way the soul speaks, and how we must find another language. I've been troubled by this from the beginning. I was accused very early on by one of the London SAP [Society of Analytical Psychology] people about my writing that I was really literary and not psychological, and that has bugged me for a long, long time, because now I've come to the conclusion that psychological language does do damage, it isn't really language of the soul. In literature, if you read Trollope or Jane Austen, it doesn't matter, these nineteenth-century novels that people read and which contained their psyche. How did the housewives of the nineteenth century contain their crazy psyches in their oppressed conditions of being women in the nineteenth century? They read novels, they had backgrounds, they had stories, in which they could hold what was happening to them, they had figures. That's what's missing.

SS: I see those as what I call providing rich articulations of experience.

JH : Good language!

SS: The question is not simply an account of an experience but articulating within its own terms. An account of an experience itself is not enlightening—a narrative, a case history, or a diary account. What great novelists did—

JH Even second-rate novels.

SS —was to provide what we're talking about, to allow experience to articulate itself in its own terms. To find fitting expression.

JH: And refinement. The subtleties of feeling were in these books. The subtleties of depression were in these books.

SS: This also links back to Jung's own practice, because what strikes me in reading accounts of Jung's practice or even Jung's procedure in the seminar is someone who had no need of psychodynamics, of developmental psychology, because he had a wealth of stories at his disposal. He was a great storyteller. I remember Mrs. Hoerni saying that he offered you the same stories, and each time they'd get better, the sense that to any situation someone brought he had a story that he could bring to bear upon it from myth, from folklore, from his own experience.

JH: Excellent! From a case, from whatever.

SS: And if he didn't he would make it up, as any good storyteller does. He would elaborate something that would enable someone to look at their experience, to mirror it, in a particular way.

JH: And to hear it differently.

SS: Yes, there was no need for one template of development—the serpent says that "the becoming of the soul follows a serpentine path,"[78] it's serpentine, it's not linear. This is an absolutely critical realization, that there's not one direct procession, and in the same way he finds himself perpetually reinstructed in different manners. In his own practice he used historical examples to do that. Part of the issue—I see it in terms of what happened historically—is that to practice like this needed that type of mind.

JH: That would be why people said you have to see Jung to do Jungian psychology.

SS: Yes. In the same way, he could dispense with psychodynamics because he's got this encyclopedic knowledge of mythology, folklore, comparative religion, and he was a great storyteller. What is amplification, in its essence, but storytelling? An exchange of storytelling. A way to highlight aspects where someone comes in with what appears to be an isolated—

JH: A unique "to me" experience.

SS: He says "That reminds me of . . ."

JH: You find yourself also in the story.

SS: It's a parallel, it's not an explanation.

JH: No, it's analogous. But this is also supposedly the way of poetic thinking, and metaphorical thinking, it's a parallel. This is also the old way of teaching with parables too. Now we have two things. One is the therapy, the isolating effect of therapy, so that the weight of human history is not carried, and the second is the self.

SS: And narrative.

JH: Yes, narrative ties in with the therapy. Let's begin with the narrative, because we were talking about Jung telling stories to his patients, and if I tell a story to a patient today in therapy it has to be understood in terms of the transference, the relationship between us. So that if the patient tells me a story I can't tell a story back, because that's interfering in the patient's objectivity of the work, and my response had better be "I wonder why you're telling me this." Or if I tell the story—"What does that remind you of"—all those kinds of things that connect us more intimately into our personal relationship called the transference. So the weight of human history is gone.

SS: It seems to me that what is operative in many forms of therapy is a form of deconstruction of narrative, which is quite the opposite of Jung's procedure.

JH: How do you mean "deconstruction of narrative"?

SS: Well you have it first in Freud in that behind any story you tell is the master plot of Oedipus, so that the stories that are told are simply disguises, masks to be unmasked, to be deciphered, as to the master plot. Now my sense with Jung is that there is no master plot. He breaks with that monomyth. There's a plurality of myths, a plurality of templates and, as we were saying, amplification is a mode of storytelling.

JH: Then I might amplify it by referring to a further story, or an image in alchemy, or an image from the movies, something that enriches it, brings it out louder, adds to the value of the story.

SS: Highlight certain aspects of it as salient, as significant, tincture it in certain ways.

JH: Or telling a parallel story allows the patient to discover a particular part that coincides.

SS: And find a different resolution, possibly to move in a different way in a situation of conflict, to envisage new possibilities.

JH: Good. And not tied to your and my emotional connections. You see, that's the problem, it releases the person to the story, and that changes your feeling about who you are. You're part of a story, and that's different.

SS: The narrative is respected, it's not deconstructed. It's not pulled apart as to what you really mean is x, y, z.

JH: What do you really mean, and why are you telling me this?

SS: Which stops the narrative. It's a great showstopper if there ever was one!

JH: And what does it remind you of, and so on and so forth. How do you feel when you tell me this story? That's a big one.

SS: Or these figures really are . . .

JH: These figures really are you and me or these figures really are your father and yourself or your mother and so on. Now, by removing the patient from the story, or deconstructing the story in the sense of devaluing the story, where is the patient left?

SS: In isolation. They're left even without their own narrative. The narrative is taken away.

JH: No, there's a problem here. The narrative the patient comes with does need a certain deconstruction, because that's part of the patient's problem, that he believes the narrative.

SS: But Jung's method is to move it on, not by reductively taking it apart.

JH: Okay, by moving it on. Even actually, literally, how does the story unfold?

SS: To enable someone to envisage new possibilities. To imagine new ways of consideration.

JH: Or to imagine the story itself as a fiction in which you are, so that you begin to imagine yourself as a piece of a story, and that is different than imagining yourself as apart from "I tell you my story." There's something very different about feeling that I'm being lived by a story.

SS: And also that that story is connected to other stories. It's connected to human history and culture.

JH: Yes, connected to human history and culture. That's the amplification. That's what amplification can do.

SS: It takes someone out of solipsism.

JH: Yes, and that's the modern suffering. That's *the* modern suffering. Being only an individual. And then along comes Jung with the individuation process, which is to understand the idea that you go into yourself and you see what can happen.

SS: The issue is not to become a windowless monad but simply to get out of yourself, reconnecting through one's own depths. That's Jung's intention.

JH: That's what I meant by the personal. The deeply personal is not subjective.

SS: This is why Jung's term "the self" is, in a certain sense, the most unfortunate term he could have used for what he intended.

JH: Hear hear!

SS: In a certain sense it's closer to another word that I dislike for different reasons, in terms of philosophical connotations, the "Other." There's nothing less close to one's self than what Jung calls the self. "Other" would have been nearer to it, but we don't want to get into the Lacanian, Sartrean thing about the "Other," we want to avoid that.

JH: Because the "Other," as I understand the way it's used now, is a result of being so trapped into the "me" that everything is the "Other." But there is no "Other," if you're not in the me. It's all permeable. So let's leave that one.

SS: It's an unfortunate coinage for, if you look at what he intended to say, he did intend to indicate something about alterity in the larger sense of the word.

JH: Yes, that there's more to my entirety than what I think is me. And that more is the self.

SS: And that's what I should submit to. And also to realize that there are larger patterns at work that ultimately escape human understanding, as you put it. Self, as he says, is in part a transcendental term, it's beyond rational explanation. So what moves us inevitably escapes us, and we need to respect that mystery.

JH: Yes, but that is also terribly abstract. It can be imagined then as the Godhead, or the spirit, and all kinds of things. That's why the weight of human history, this wonderful phrase at the very beginning of our talk, and that you talk about, is so important, because that's the larger real, so to speak, thing that encompasses me, instead of the word "self."

SS: But the question there is what does one do with it? It's the question of the burden of history and Jung in certain problematic ways puts a direction to history in that he does see some teleological principle in play, there's a soteriology in his undertaking.

JH: That's a subject that requires a lot of separate thinking, because is it Jung who does this, or is there something about events or images that want to go beyond themselves, that are implications, and that this thrust in the image to imply beyond itself would be the movement that you're speaking about rather than the person. So if you're dealing with images, they *imply*, they're like seeds that have lines going out from them.

SS: I think that clearly is one aspect, that historically speaking in Jung individuation is a soteriological process, that is, it finds its ultimate sanction and meaning and import in the process of divine self-revelation. But it is quite solidly in Jung's framework to remain within Judeo-Christianity. That's how he frames it. In a certain sense, he folds it back within a particular religious tradition.

JH: Well a lot of this is the whole Christian line that follows Jung and wants to emphasize that, so that individuation is a path of salvation even. I don't know if that's the main thrust, though, I really don't, and if it is I certainly find the entire progressivism very disturbing, very idealistic in its effects on people, in the way it's written about and talked about. I'm talking now about the second generation, the third generation, and so on. It moves away from things as they are, the "confrontation," such a big word in Jung, *Auseinandersetzung* with what is.

SS: One finds in quite a striking way this concern with soteriology within contemporary culture. Witness the concern with global warming, the notion that if I use an aerosol I'm endangering the survival of the planet. This need to feel connected with the fate of something larger I find quite extraordinary.

JH: *Tikkun olam*, which is the restoration of the fallen world.

SS: It goes beyond: I recycle because I think it's the right thing to do. This need to feel the weight of rescuing the planet, like everyone is an Atlas, upon whom the fate of the world depends, I find extraordinary.

JH: Let's say this redemption urge is some sort of given with our nature, and the question is where does it get put in different periods of history. It seems now to be put into the greening of the planet.

SS: And I think one has to be very careful about this because people are now using science, or whatever science they read in the newspapers, to construct a new cosmology and soteriology.

JH: I want to go back for a minute to this use of the word "self," because I find that if the modern condition is cut-offness from the world, cut-offness from others, from the community, from nature and all the rest, the dead world of Descartes, we are more and more individual and more and more alone, more and more isolated—*anomie*, as a French sociologist called it—then how in the world can Jungian psychology offer a solution, since it talks so much about individuation?

SS: In that regard "individuation" is also not necessarily the best chosen word. He adopted it from Schopenhauer and von Hartmann because it depicts, in Jung's understanding, a passage away from solipsism.

JH: That's how Jung understands it.

SS: That's the whole point. It's an opening to the contemporary world, an opening to the dead and to history.

JH: It's the opening to the dead and the deeply personal. And the deeply personal is connecting back through history, it's connecting to all that's been left out and forgotten. So it's not individuation in that sense. The process is one of connection or restoration or remembrance. Why don't we call it that? The process of remembering. Anamnesis.

SS: A recollection in an almost Platonic sense.

JH: That would be perfect for what the work is.

SS: For recollecting the forms that animate us.

JH: Recollecting the forms that animate us, the forms that are neglected, forgotten, and feared. Mainly feared. Not ours. Somehow in therapy the idea that what you discover is part of you, part of the self, even if Jung doesn't mean it that way, but the very fact that we think these are parts of the self, for the greater wholeness of the person, these are all inflating ways of seeing what's happening.

SS: In a way, in historical practice, in a broader sense, this type of conception is essential. The whole endeavor of historical practices, in the way that I see it, is to historicize the present, to indicate: look, what appears to be intractable should be reconceived in a different way and you can then, as it were, loosen something intractable by indicating that this has a certain historicity.

JH: By getting into its history?

SS: Yes, by retracing its formation its contingency can be revealed. New ways of thinking can be generated, so *that* to me is what I see as the significance of the history of psychology.

JH: This is lovely, because this makes the historian the therapist. History is the therapy. I like that.

SS: This is what it attempts to do, to open a way of considering the constitution of a state we're in.

JH: So that's a historical analysis.

SS: Yes.

JH: I'm using the word "analysis" in the analysis of what that constitution is, then that revisions it.

SS: It opens new possibilities and it also opens up the possibility of reclamation. One is able to show, for instance, that what appears in psychology as contemporary issues are not in the least bit contemporary, that some of the brightest minds at the end of the nineteenth century were grappling with the self-same problems.

JH: If they're the real problems, they're being dealt with again and again and again, that's the beauty of the historian. That's a tremendous moment to close this little chapter, understanding that the historian is the therapist. There's something to tell the therapists, who are not very happy with the historian taking over the *Red Book* and exposing the *Red Book* and showing what the *Red Book* is to the world. This is not a historical thing for them, this is nothing to do with the history, that's all just facts and incidentals. What matters is the therapy. Well the therapy is the actual therapy of our world today, which the public evidently realizes, because hundreds, thousands of copies are being bought and carried home with people. They must recognize that this bit of history, which is the *Red Book*, is their therapy, the therapy of our time.

SS: And it gives them a new way to envisage their issues. They are connected with something that one would have considered to be utterly remote.

JH: It couldn't be more remote.

SS: There's the man tracking his fantasies by Lake Zurich, transcribing them in an ornate Gothic script for sixteen years . . .

JH: With figures from the gnostic and arcane past, everything is so absurd and radical and peculiar and weird. That is the arcane to what's missing in the culture. History as therapy.

SS: And possibly, as Umberto Eco put it, bringing people back to a certain Middle Ages that is still present.[79]

JH: Ah, but not in full atavism. There's a ridiculous love of the Middle Ages or the Elizabethan period, you know, but none of that. It's not the literal Middle Ages, it's something else, a certain attitude, in which there was a cosmology that embraced it all.

FIFTH CONVERSATION

JH: The *Red Book* is important even for people who don't know really why it's important. It's an icon of something. It seems to me that it restructures, or deconstructs, or changes—whatever we want to call it—the idea of the profoundly personal. The deep subjectivity. It turns out what's profoundly personal in this book is *not* one's personal life, the depths of one's childhood, the trauma, the family: all of that isn't what Jung encounters in the depths. He encounters human history. He encounters figures, he encounters the imagination, and *that's* the profoundly personal, that frees me, or anyone, it frees me from this constant introspection, getting hold of what's really wrong with me, how I developed this way, what's my personality, what's my trauma. Instead of all of that introspective disease of the last hundred years, *cogito ergo sum*, I think therefore I am, so all my introspective thinking leads me to who I am: *no*. What you discover is that what's in the depths is human history, and figures and creatures and scenes and landscapes and voices and instruction and an extraordinary world, that's the depth of personality, and it makes me no longer psychological. I'm no longer caught in the hundred years of Western psychology.

SS: What Jung hits upon is a stream of images and he encounters collective memory and fantasy. It's not personal memory. There is a mnemonic dimension there, but he finds that what is animated, what is critical there, is collective memory. He finds himself having to address debates such as that between the Christian and the pagan and to see then how that reframes his own life. It's not that his life is subtracted out of it, but the *realia*, the *personalia* of his life, isn't the fundament. It's the images that frame him.

JH: We are lived by them, as he says in other places.

SS: It's what he then realizes, that there are powers that move in his depths.

JH: That's the profoundly personal.

SS: You couldn't imagine a less Freudian book. It just completely bursts that framework.

JH: Which dominated the last hundred years. We've had a hundred years of psychotherapy based on introspection. And this is not introspective, this is an account, this is a *récit*, in Corbin's sense, a kind of visionary journey through a world of scenes, a world of places, a world of people, of figures. That's not achievable through introspection.[80]

SS: Or it's introspection where the viewers themselves change in the act of viewing. It's not constant: he's allowing himself, his perspective, to be shifted, quite radically.

JH: In fact he's a participant.

SS: He's allowing himself to enter into the drama, the scene of the fantasies as one participant among others.

JH: He's a member of the *dramatis personae*. He's in the cast.

SS: One amongst others.

JH: Yes, one among others. Now isn't that a huge insight just to begin with? Isn't that a huge relief for the egocentric human being of our time, who goes to his therapy and tries to work out his problems, when *this* says you're one among others. There are a lot of people in your house. You don't live alone.

SS: And transformations happen to this "I." The "I" becomes a greening being, a chameleon, it undergoes fantastic transformations. It's not a fixed human being—

JH: —with a particular point of view. And it has to suffer challenges to everything this "I" brings.

SS: The sharpest example of that is at the beginning of *Scrutinies*, where Jung has this confrontation with the "I," which suddenly shifts. My "I," I have to live with you. How am I going to continue with this other entity?[81]

JH: Now, just there we can translate that event into the language he uses in what you might call his conceptual work as relativization of the ego. That's a term he uses, or it becomes that way in English anyway. And that phrase doesn't carry anything, it's an abstraction that doesn't give the right value to what it really feels like.

SS: Paradoxically, if you're talking about relativizing the ego, the ego still remains in the central position, although its position is being decentered, relativized, and so forth, whereas what is evocative about this *Scrutinies* section is the "I" is itself personified. He sits and talks to his "I," addresses his "I." So the question is who is doing the addressing? It's left open.

JH: I always thought, Who was doing the questioning? I thought in my own way of describing this long before I found the *Red Book*—the "I" is a scribe. He's an accountant, or he's a note taker or something, that's all. He's just the court reporter, somebody who notes it down, because the "I" that's really in the game is the one the court reporter is reporting on, the one under attack.

SS: I think that's appropriate in this instance, because what is going on the whole time is a writing. This is taking place within writing.

JH: So then we could begin to talk about writing, but I wonder if we want to do that, since both of us do that. That's a theme of its own. I don't know if I want to do that. But do you see, it's not just that we pass or leave the book, nothing could be more non-Freudian. It's that it is a tremendous relief of the sense of guilt or responsibility for everything that's happened in my life as being *my* doing, and therefore *my* rectification, through insight, through introspection, through working on my analysis, seeing my therapist, working through the transference, all the various things that people have been doing for a hundred years. Instead you're engaged with what you call this flow or stream of deep psychic life, which is at the same time a stream of energy, because this kept Jung going for fifteen years. It wasn't only the rituals of his daily life, family, military, patients. It was this *liveliness* of the stream.

SS: It not only kept him going, he found his orientation through it. He found his reason for being and it structured his world.

JH: It answered that very question he began with, which is loss of soul, what is my myth, who am I? That question, who am I, what am I here for, what are we to do, what am *I* to do, the figures appear. They don't give him a clear message: "You are to be this or that." They engage him in such a way that he finds what to do in the doing. This is what he is to do.

SS: There's a moment in *The Secret of the Golden Flower* when he speaks about the realization of the significance of letting things happen, of "Gelassenheit," which he says is a lesson that Meister Eckhart taught him, analogous to the *wu wei* of the Taoists, of allowing psychic events to happen of their own accord.[82] The relativization happens straight off there, which is allowing the spontaneous emergence of figures, stepping back, and then attempting to take stock, to follow what ensues.

JH: And he gives credit to what comes. I think that's really an important aspect of the attitude. He's upset, and he resists, and all those various immediate reactions, because he says you must take these things literally, and if some shocking image appears you have to react as you would in daily life to it, but he gives credit to what appears.

SS: There's a very powerful ethic there, of respect for the figures and situations that he finds himself in. His immediate assumption, throughout these scenes, these dialogues, is not that he is right. His immediate assumption is that he is wrong and that the figures and situations will instruct him.

JH: They know more than he does.

SS: Yes. And he has to break his head for years to figure out what. He's not bringing to bear a fixed set of positions.

JH: That's very important. He sets them aside, like that phenomenologist *epoché* [suspension]. He brackets out all that he knows, his fixed positions.

SS: This is his opening gambit. Let us assume that these figures have something to teach. He may be completely wrong but he's willing to take that risk. He's willing to take the risk of the complete and utter foolishness and ridiculousness of his undertaking. And one finds that expressed at a certain point toward the end of *Liber Secundus*—his soul has fled up to Heaven, his God has been reborn as the son of the frogs, and he thinks Philemon is a charlatan that's just duped him and he's just sitting there, but he sits there.[83] He is willing to bear the foolishness of doing nothing other than, night after night, going down and entering—this is where he is in his life and there's nothing other for him to do than to pick up these fragments of fantasy and enter into the maelstrom again and again and again. He says this is distasteful to him, in the 1925 seminar, as a rational thinker.[84] What on earth is he getting himself into. This is a tremendous scholar who could well have carried on in that vein for the rest of his life, writing something akin to Frazer's *Golden Bough* from a psychological angle, ten volumes of *Transformations and Symbols of the Libido*, and got himself a chair at some university. But that's dead. He reenters scholarship, but from a completely different angle. His scholarly enterprise subsequent to that is to give flesh, to give context to his own inner experience.

JH: And this own inner experience is not his. This is where these figures are actual figures in a curious way from the literature, from history. Salome is a figure, Philemon has a background. So he is also showing that what lies in the depths of the human being—and he then is an example of a human being who has gone into these depths, which is the great classical move from Dante and so on—is what does not belong to him, not part of his personal life, and yet is profoundly personal and addressed to him. That's a paradox. And the lesson that we draw or that he is proposing is that this is everybody's, that there is something universal about this. If you or I do the same thing we will encounter figures, we will encounter scenes, we will encounter human history. I think that's a lesson. Do you think so?

SS: Well that's then the project he embarks on, in that maybe this isn't just purely idiosyncratic.

JH: Yes, this is not a case.

SS: And he then tries to replicate that in his patients.

JH: Right. I remember I corresponded with Tina Keller, when she was a very old woman in her nineties—she was instructed by him in the early 1920s—on how to proceed with active imagination.[85]

SS: It was a collective experiment. He wanted to see if the same thing would happen with other people.

JH: And then he makes the parallels through written text and so on and so forth. But there's one great difference between what he does and what others have done. We've talked about this, you and I, several times. The fact that the universality of it, that this is possible for everyone, doesn't mean that this is a universal system or method or program. In other words, he doesn't take the content of what's said to him and make that prophecy or proclaim it.

SS: There's a double tension. I think that initially he starts down that track, it's self-styled as a prophetic work, but the aspect most specific to his undertaking is that he steps back from it. He becomes skeptical of his own visions. There's one point where he says you're not significant because you see something significant.

JH: That's holy. You are not significant just because you see something significant.

SS: Yes, don't confuse yourself with a vision. And I think this is one reason why he holds back from publishing the work, because his skepticism at a philosophical level comes back in. This is why he becomes interested in, you could say, the psychology of the vision-making process.

JH: You wrote that he is more interested in the psychological function that does this than in what is produced.

SS: He could have set up shop as a prophet, had he so wished.

JH: You see, this question comes up with many people who get in touch with that stream. They then set up shop as a prophet. They're convinced by what they've encountered. It's utterly real, utterly powerful, utterly true, and it needs to be told. It comes with its own impetus. But he remained a psychologist in part, that tension you speak of. So he wants to understand the workings of this.

SS: William James speaks of this in *The Varieties of Religious Experience*. His expression is "experiences that become authoritative for an individual," this immanent authority.[86] What is critical for Jung is he steps back from regarding that as authoritative for someone else. His task then, as he sees it, is to assist individuals in acquiring, in experiencing something, in their own way, that is authoritative for them but not binding upon others.

JH: And the content will be different. You see that problem came up way back when I wrote the commentary to Gopi Krishna's Kundalini experience,[87] because Gopi Krishna was delighted that I would undertake the task of getting his diaries, his experience, published and I wrote a commentary that constantly says what he experienced and how he understood his experience, how it looks from another point of view. When the book was finished, and he read the whole thing, he was not happy at all because he wanted the message of his experience to be transmitted, the literal message of the transformation of the mind through the uprising of the Kundalini, and so on and so forth. He didn't want to raise a question—he used the word "skeptic"—and saw it as skeptical. He didn't see it as another level of understanding. Yes, there's this message, but there's also a world in which you can put this message into parallels, into functions of the psyche, even into psychiatric diagnoses about delusions and so on. In other words, he didn't want any kind of *doubt* put in there. Now Jung comes out of the Protestant tradition, and doubt is a very important function. He remains, I think, a true Christian in doubting even as he believes.

SS: That's the signature trait of the book. Books of revelation or personal transformation, resolving faith and a particular worldview, are two a penny. To step back from generating a worldview out of immediate experience . . . I'll restart that. Books in which an individual undergoes a transformative experience and lead to conviction, into a certain set of principles, a worldview or cosmology, are not rare. And they are evocative. But one then is left after reading such texts with a sense of, well, this was convincing for *x* but it isn't for me.

JH: Or it's convincing for a few followers. Or even many followers.

SS: If we adopt the worldview in question. The *Red Book* is a peculiar work because on the one hand it looks as if he's doing this but, on the other hand, he clearly isn't. He steps back from even believing in his own revelation, let alone taking it as legislative upon others. It self-styles as a prophetic work, this is "The Way of What Is to Come." I've experienced it.

JH: And in that high-blown language. He became aware of the high-blown language, even talks about it in his other works. In the *Collected Works* he talks about the animus using particular ways of speaking, and the anima, the inflations that come with that, so he was aware of this as he went on. He was beginning to hear it, I would say, with his psychiatric ear.

SS: I am not sure if it is psychiatric but it is a differentiation of the figures. A critical moment of the text is in *Scrutinies*, where he writes that the figure of Philemon has changed, and he comes to realize that perhaps the greater part of what he has written in the first two books, *Liber Primus* and *Liber Secundus*, had actually been given to him by Philemon.[88] *He* is not the author, there is a prophetic figure in him whom he then steps back from. There's a differentiation of the voices.

JH: That's really very important. He hears that.

SS: That's the disidentification. There's a prophetic voice in me that's not me, that's not myself.

JH: And I need to be aware of it.

SS: Not simply become its mouthpiece, its spokesman.

JH: And that's a temptation.

SS: I can learn something from it, but the issue is not simply giving over to it, ceding right of way.

JH: You say that it's in the *Scrutinies*, after the first two books, placed in the end, which is written from 1914 to 1917?

SS: The fantasies continue where he left off *Liber Secundus*, in February 1914, and it contains fantasies which run through to 1916. He writes it in the autumn of 1917. Everything in the text is complete by 1917. The transcription is then what takes him into the 1920s.

JH: So he is transcribing with emendations, and you can tell the inserts?

SS: You can. I tried to indicate the most critical ones in the notes. The emendations, strikingly, are very rarely to the depictions of the fantasies themselves. The emendations are to the second layer of commentary—a reconsideration of his own reflections on his experience—and that's what he revises.

JH: But not the direct experiences. That's what makes the book very confusing is keeping these levels separate as you go through it. You look up something, you read a few pages, and you don't know at that moment whether the pages you are reading were written later than the raw experience. This part is difficult.

SS: It took me years and years to figure it out. It was only with the *Black Books* that I could establish a chronology, and then it fit like clockwork.

JH: Because he didn't date each entry.

SS: He dated each entry in the *Black Books* and not in the *Red Book*. The problem became worse when I had a color copy of the facsimile of the calligraphic version, because there were dates in that. I later realized that the dates referred to where he had got to in the transcription or to the paintings. For five years I had no idea whether a particular section was written in 1914 or 1928, which for a historian is a complete hell.

JH: It's like medieval manuscripts or something.

SS: Yes. But once I'd established the chronology it fit together.

JH: That's a difficult thing. In other words, some of the images, the written-out pages, were transcriptions done much later but the content was actually earlier. But I think we've tried to make it pretty clear, at least it's clear to me, the significance of the popular interest in this book. I think it's tremendously freeing, for instance, from the burden of what I have considered to be my personal life, and working it through.

SS: There's another aspect to it. Two other aspects. The first is I've had people write letters saying, I thought I was the only one out there who had such fantasies. This is a tremendous validation to the type of material that is far more common than one realizes. The other aspect is for individuals to read a book like this and see that there is a figure such as Jung with a degree of culture, sophistication, intellectual brilliance, and this is what he had to do to figure himself out, and to find his own place in the world, and it gives them courage. If that's what *he* had to do, it gives *me* courage.

JH: That's very good. The fact that so many people have their visions, and have unexpected experiences, is always regarded as idiosyncratic and, in some way or another, anecdotal only if it rises into a cult in some way, that the person identifies with the material and becomes prophetic and has a following, gets it out in some form. Otherwise it's private, and the only way, or form or box, we can put it in in our culture is that it's private and it's delusional and an invasion, an incursion of a latent psychosis or at best Ellenberger's term, a creative illness.[89] I think we should take exception to that idea, that Jung had and went through a creative illness. I don't see how you can call what he had an illness. I don't think the term "illness" is benefited by giving it an adjective called "creative."

SS: It's still within a pathological framework.

JH: Exactly. So that needs to be addressed. We need to take this question up, because this is what embarrasses the people who don't want to see the book published, because, look, it shows Jung's creative illness! Jung went through a period of breakdown and some sort of minor psychosis.

SS: The text itself stages this in the chapter *Liber Secundus*, called "Nox Secunda," where Jung's "I" finds himself in a lunatic asylum and diagnosed as suffering from religious paranoia simply because he's reading Thomas à Kempis's *The Imitation of Christ* and protests that he never felt better.[90] So he's critically aware of this form of reading.

JH: Did he know the Schreber case at that time?

SS: Yes, he did. If you look at Jung's life during this period, his correspondences, his professional activities—1914 to 1920—it's clear to me that he keeps a strict partition between his own experimentation and all other aspects of his life. It doesn't bleed over in the least. I've simply found no sign of anything that either a contemporary, someone living in that time, or today—

JH: —would have said that this man's off his rocker!

SS: Retrospective diagnosis is something historians don't engage in. But one is aware of what the categories were at that time. So, for instance, if he'd spoken to Eugen Bleuler, or Emil Kraepelin, he's engaging in a controlled experiment. He's not stripping naked and running round the lake.

JH: No, and he's also not pronouncing these things that are happening. He doesn't make prophetic pronouncements to the world. At the most, he's telling a selected few people, perhaps employing some of the things he's discovered as active imagination within his practice, after 1916, when the Club is formed, so the whole thing is done with sagacity.

SS: And he's inviting editorial comment from his circle.

JH: I didn't know about that. Explain it a bit.

SS: He wants dispassionate eyes to look at it, dispassionate eyes to look over it.

JH: He did pass out the *Seven Sermons.*

SS: *Seven Sermons* was privately published in a pseudonymous form in 1916. He gave that to friends.

JH: And he didn't give this out with the intention of conversion. I think he gave it with the intention that this is something valuable.

SS: I think it was also a test case for how the publication of the whole thing could work.

JH: Already then?

SS: Already then. He's testing out his audience.

JH: Because it must have bugged him, thinking what am I going to do with all this?

SS: It's written for publication, that's clear. But he remains ambivalent about the form of publication.

JH: Well, he wasn't doing it in the calligraphy at the time.

SS: He was, in 1916.

JH: By 1916 he was? But it was originally typed, wasn't it? Or handwritten first in the notebooks.

SS: Handwritten, then typed, and then retranscribed. He started it in 1915. So it's intended for publication. One thinks what would have happened in his circle if in 1921 it wasn't *Psychological Types* that was published but *Liber Novus*, the *Red Book*. A whole different history.

JH: That's like those questions that come up, you know, if Lee had won the Civil War, or if Hitler had done so and so, I mean if *that* book had been published rather than the other book what would have happened? You get this whole new imaginary history.

What you said the other day seems to me very important, that what was the great discovery in the depths is the imagination. We've been talking about it in terms of prophecy, we've been talking about it in terms of the figures and the landscapes and all, but actually what he reestablished was that the psyche is a living world of imagination and that any person can descend into that world. That's your truth, that's what you are, that's what your soul is. You're in search of a soul, and your soul is imagination. As Blake said, Jesus, the imagination, meaning the very creative power, the redemptive power, the strength that you are, is given to you by this remarkable thing that Coleridge called the esemplastic imagination, this force that presents itself figured.[91] They are your teachers, they are your motivators, and they are your landscapes. That's what the habitations of your depths are. This seems to me the prophecy. I think this is the teaching that *does* come out.

SS: Is it prophecy or is it rather where he finds himself? There's a temptation to turn it into prophecy, to take certain symbolic utterances in a literal way.

JH: Yes, that's the general view of prophecy, but I'm using David Miller's idea that the prophet was not foretelling, but forth-telling, meaning telling it like it is.[92] This is who you are, you are floating, you are part of the living stream of imagination. When that's lost by the contemporary psychologists, or discounted, or seen as illness or anything else, they're losing the basic message that Jung gave us through this.

SS: One sees it in the work, but I'm wondering if that would have been enough for him.

JH: He wants some of the message to come through.

SS: I think he's reaching beyond that, reaching for a transcendental dimension. Although what he's actually showing throughout is a practice of the image.

JH: That's what he's showing, the practice of the image, yes.

SS: But he's always reaching beyond it.

JH: And yet he says this is my work, don't try to imitate what I'm doing, and so on and so forth. He tries to pull people back from reaching for or copying that transcendental vision. It's tricky.

SS: That is one of the dynamic tensions that structures the whole work.

JH: Well, you're able to hold that. You keep us in that tension, but it's so easy to go off into the transcendental and follow Jung's attempt to reconfigure the Godhead. That's a big thing.

SS: It's like the Edinger line of Jung as the third revelation.[93]

JH: Yes, that Jung truly is the third revelation.

SS: I don't think that's how Jung saw himself.

JH: Or you can go another way and say this is a psychotic episode, full of delusional material, which Jung, because he was smart, knew how to make a certain picture of and deal with, but it shouldn't have been published because it's an embarrassment, it just proves this idea of creative illness. You see what happens? It can go in these different ways. But you've kept the tension. You keep the fact of these extremes that people want to reduce it to, to a masterwork, in which the tension is exactly what makes it a masterwork.

SS: That is what is compelling about it. It is the most worked, elaborated text in Jung's canon. Paradoxically there's more spontaneity in terms of the writing in many of his manuscripts. For instance, there's a thirty-page manuscript called "African Voyage"—it's clearly written at the top, "African Voyage"—and he intended to write about Africa—

JH: This is after his trip?

SS: After his trip. And the bulk of it is on his visit to the Pueblos in Taos. He stops off there and never returns to the main theme, so there's more automaticity in his scholarly writings than in this. There's nothing that compares to the careful reworking and editing of individual sentences.

JH: Really? That you would see just by looking at the manuscripts? The actual sentences are carefully revised, as a poet would do.

SS: Constantly reworked over a period of sixteen years. This is a work. To echo something Maurice Blanchot wrote, madness is the *absence* of work.[94]

JH: Madness is the absence of work, and this is a piece of tremendous work, a masterwork.

SS: This is the most laboriously worked item in Jung's corpus.

SIXTH CONVERSATION

JH: Even if we have somehow dealt with this attack from the
side of conventional psychiatry—that it's not a creative illness
or an illness of any sort—there's another attack on this book,
which comes from the Christian side. This work that Jung does
is demonic, really demonic, in the modern sense of demons.
Karl Jaspers says so and lists five reasons why this going into the
underworld and talking with figures and listening to voices, and
doing what Jung did, is demonic, it's non-Christian.[95] It opens
the door to the chaos that Christ, by telling his followers that his
voice—that's the official thing—is the only voice to listen to. The
only voice you ever hear is the voice of Jesus. I'm saying this badly
but I think you know what I mean. This book is attacked on the
one hand by psychiatry and conventional orthodoxy and, on the
other hand, by conventional orthodoxy from Christianity. What
about that attack?

SS: It *is* an heretical text. But it remains within a Christian
framework.

JH: It remains within a Christian framework. Oh, very much so,
yes.

SS: If there were an index, it would show that the critical figure is
Christ. In Jung's later writings, the development of the Christian
tradition led to a suppression of what he calls individual symbol
formation, so that it had blocked access to direct religious

experience. This was what he saw his whole endeavor as recovering.

JH: And it is therapeutic.

SS: So in terms of what we spoke of earlier, of the encounter with the weight of history, he's dealing with the sequelae, the effects of two centuries of Christianity upon the soul.

JH: You mean two millennia?

SS: Yes, two millennia. He's dealing with the effect of two millennia of Christianity upon the soul. He'll take this up in 1923 in his seminars at Polzeath, where he speaks of the four great repressions by ecclesiastical Christianity: repression of the *animal*, repression of the *natural man*, repression of *individual symbol formation*, and repression of *nature*.[96] That's in his seminars in Polzeath in 1923, giving particular significance to repression of individual symbol formation. This then is directly connected with his interest in Gnosticism, because in his view he saw Gnosticism as the one area that preserved individual symbol formation within a Christian framework. So what he engages with is a daimonology, something that opens up to other traditions—one has Egyptian, Greek, and Hindu Gods populating the text and that's an important dimension to it.

JH: And figures unheralded. Not necessarily figures that belong to one or another tradition, just voices.

SS: His own iconography. You once wrote a paper on Jung's daimonic inheritance, which I think highlighted that aspect.[97]

JH: Exactly. He did call up voices from the deep, and these are daimons, in the Greek sense of the word, and I believe in the *Red Book* you keep that spelling, "daimon," right?

SS: We had a lot of discussion on that issue.

JH: Because these were figures from the middle world. They were not necessarily only from the underworld. They were the mediators in a way but they were living figures. The Neoplatonists had many others, they had archons and so on and so forth, and the Roman Catholic tradition embodied many kinds of figures. But this daimonic inheritance is objected to, as I started off to say earlier, and I used Karl Jaspers as the example of saying that this is where Jung betrays Christianity and the revelation of Christ. Other voices—"Get thee behind me, Satan"—are not to be listened to, they're tempters.

SS: In Jung's view, recovering the full depth and range of individual symbol formation is the way forward, paradoxically, to the revivification of Christianity.

JH: In that he's a Protestant, isn't he? Isn't that what Protestants wanted, and that's why there were so many kinds of Protestants?

SS: He sees that's what's been lost in Protestantism.

JH: Been lost?

SS: Been lost, individual symbol formation. There's a correspondence with his friend and colleague Adolf Keller. I think it's after reading *Answer to Job*, Keller says if you keep on in this vein you've gone over to the Catholic side. He accuses him of crypto-Catholicism.[98] What's striking about Jung's psychology of religion is that he focuses on such issues as the Mass and dogma, issues that are not exactly the most prominent within Protestantism.[99]

JH: Or the Trinity.[100]

SS: He tries to recover at a hermeneutic dimension that had been lost. Specifically, what had been lost in terms of the richness of symbolic expression.

JH: I still would say that the impulse in him is a Protestant impulse.

SS: It only makes sense within the Protestant framework. Also that opening to other traditions as well.

One of the most striking statements in the work, which we've touched on already, is in one of the drafts where he indicates, "Not one item of the Christian law is abrogated, but instead we are adding a new one: accepting the lament of the dead."[101]

JH: The lament of the dead?

SS: The lament of the dead. The dead are not only Christian.

JH: That is where the heresy occurs. That's where his being is letting in—

SS: —the dead of human history.

JH: Pagans.

SS: Nor is it simply then a question of conversion.

JH: Letting them in, in order to convert them.

SS: Yes, as according to the apocryphal gospels this took place with Christ's descent into Hell—he preached in Hell.

JH: Is it an ecumenical move of his? Let's get it all together in one church?

SS: There is clearly an opening toward that.

JH: It seems to me it's deeper. That seems like solving the problem of opposites by taking in a little bit of everything.

SS: There is a validation of revelation per se, regardless of any canonical formulation. So is "ecumenical" the right word? As I understand it, ecumenical still means people remain within a specific tradition, but it becomes an opening to a situation of respect for others. If one for instance takes one of the epochal events, the 1893 world congress of religions in Chicago, gatherings of representatives from all various religious traditions, during the proceedings they each gave their talks with respect for others but there was no shift within each position.[102] In that sense Jung is clearly sympathetic to such tolerance, which was a movement that again his friend Adolf Keller was instrumental in, but that's not where Jung is putting his energy.

JH: He would rather there were some shift within orthodox or traditional Christianity?

SS: Yes, that's more radical, because in his view this stream of images, this stream of figures, is what was at base of all religions. What comes first in his view is an inner experience of this, an experience of the stream, which then became formalized—ultimately, one could say dogmatized—in various traditions.

JH: And in that sense the dead are lamenting, because in some curious way they have not been allowed in.

SS: No. So what is critical is trying to draw near to the experiences at the base of various religious traditions. It's Jung's interest in what I call the psychology of the religion-making process. How are religions made?

JH: In other words, the religious function, as he sometimes calls it.

SS: In the Terry lectures.[103]

JH: That's very interesting. Say that again. He's interested in how religions form to begin with. Out of what do they come? What is this function of the soul that produces religion, or what is the function of the Gods within a religion?

SS: How are religions made? He looks to his own experience to give an inkling of it. His view is that religions are built up from an initial experience of a stream of images, and then only subsequently formalized into creeds, dogmas, and institutions. But the stream is one, and it is at the base of all religions.

JH: That's a very interesting idea.

SS: It is a radical idea. It's beyond ecumenicalism.

JH: And it's also beyond the individual prophet, who's given from God the holy text, the word. It's not that. It's not a word given by a Godhead.

SS: No. It valorizes individual experience, in all its particularities.

JH: That's fine. Again, that's his root Protestantism.

SS: Precisely.

JH: So he's not heretic at all. He's standing for the right, for the individual's religious experience.

SS: That is the development of Protestantism in the nineteenth century. And it remains a bedrock for him, taken one stage further into valorizing what is at base of other religious traditions.

JH: All the way through, the flavor in the book, and the word "Christ" is so often in the book, as is the Godhead, he's wrestling with his inheritance, he's wrestling with his actual father, he's wrestling with the Church, he's wrestling with the world he grew up in, with nineteenth-century Christianity as he knew it in Switzerland and with theologians. Yet despite all that, as you have always been pointing out, there's tension in Jung. He doesn't throw it out. He finds a way to remain with Christ. In his later written work he brings in the assumption of Mary, he brings in Job and another view of the need for the humanizing of God.[104] There's so much more he does later on, but still he remains, I think, a member of the Christian religion.

SS: That's what he specifically states. In the 1930s, he says that he stands on the extreme left wing of Protestantism.[105]

JH: Extreme left wing of Protestantism? Quite explicit.

SS: His dead, or prominent among his dead, are the Christian dead, his own forefathers, and that is part of the inheritance and legacy he grapples with. The task that he then takes up is one of revivifying ecclesiastical Christianity. Now, as I see it, his later writings on these topics are already there as conceptions in the *Red Book*. So what one finds in *Answer to Job*, with respect to the reformulation of the Judeo-Christian God image, is based on the figural ground of his theophany of the figure of Abraxas. It certainly is a God experience, of a God that encompasses all contraries, including evil.

JH: Yes, it's the crucial part.

SS: That's already there. But it takes him decades to reapproach this from the side of scholarship and theological history. The fire and the power in that book is this immediacy of his own theophany, of the figural ground. As he says, in a note in the *Black Books*, Abraxas is the uniting of the Christian God with Satan.[106] It's reincorporating evil into the Godhead. It's the great theme of *Answer to Job*.

JH: Indeed. He refuses Manichaeism, he refuses splitting them apart, he refuses the turning evil into a *privatio boni*, just the absence of the blessings of God. That's later. He also later insists that the Godhead includes the feminine. But that's also implied in the *Red Book*, isn't it?

SS: Yes, that's there as well.

JH: His own religion was forming in the *Red Book*. His old religion was being destroyed, meaning the inherited Christianity that he felt was oppressive, if I'm right now about this, and at the same time a new vision, or a new understanding of religion, his actual religion that he developed in later work, is being given to him, or he's struggling with in the *Red Book*. It's a religious struggle that he's going through at the same time.

SS: Completely. That's what the text is, in essence.

JH: I'm interested in the urge for universality. I was thinking about how Einstein wants this unified theory that can explain the cosmos, the monotheistic urge, this desire of Freud wanting his universality of the Oedipus complex. It's a very interesting urge in people. And I think Jung doesn't have that. Or there's a tension about it.

SS: There's a tension about it. I think that the whole archetype theory is—

JH: This would be a universalism? But there are multiple archetypes, and he's never been able to give a list of all the archetypes.

SS: Still they're universal.

JH: Fire would be universal, or the sun would be universal. There's a lot of danger in that. So his comparative study of religions is actually to unearth the archetypal universals.

SS: The underlying universal process, which even as individuation he posits as a universal process.

JH: Yes, I guess that's where his work ties in with Eliade. Eliade, Scholem, and Corbin were all attacked by a university professor by the name of Wasserstrom out in Seattle, you know of that?[107]

SS: I read that book. I found it unreadable.

JH: But he found these three to be trying to set up a private religion, and that would be the same accusation they could bring against Jung.

SS: I rather see them as using their own experience to enlighten the texts they are studying. If you read, say, Eliade's text on yoga, he doesn't directly refer to his own experience but he knows whereof he speaks.[108]

JH: The same is true of Corbin. When he talked toward the end of his lectures his eyes would go up and you could feel he *was* these visions of Soharwardi, or whoever he was doing.

SS: You cannot write a text like *Avicenna and the Visionary Recital*[109] without having engaged with this.

JH: No, he *was* it. So why did this Norwegian in Seattle hate them so much?

SS: I think certain people have an allergy toward this type of writing.

JH: Very defensive about keeping the faith of the faith. Jung doesn't talk about belief, does he? William James wrote of this in *Will to Believe*,[110] and my concern with the whole problem of religion is believing, that's why I think Jung's skepticism or his doubt or his differentiation is so terribly important. He doesn't get caught in belief. But then what does he believe at the end of the work? What's the belief system? Not system, what is the belief? It's the belief in Jesus as an image of the self, the self *as* Jesus.

SS: It's Philemon who says to him, I don't believe, I teach what I know.[111]

JH: Who says that? Philemon?

SS: Yes, in *Scrutinies*. I teach what I know, I don't teach what I believe.

JH: So Jung answers that question: I don't believe, I know.

SS: It's Philemon at the back of that.

JH: That might be worth picking up, that little bit.

SS: Jung created a lot of controversy in the 1950s after the airing of John Freeman's interview, where Freeman asked Jung whether he believed in God or not, and Jung hesitated and famously replied to the effect, I don't believe, I know.[112] I see in that slight hesitation the beginning of a smile, the memory of a dialogue with Philemon forty-odd years prior. He didn't teach what he believed, he taught what he knew. That was the message that Jung learned from Philemon.

JH: It gives a much, much more acceptable response than I've been able to accept previously, because then Jung isn't saying "I know God," he's saying, "I know my experiences."

SS: "And that's all I have."

JH: "That's all I have, and I can teach my experiences." It's very different. But I don't think that's what came through, because when I've dealt with this in the classroom, people will immediately say, well, Jung believed in God. But Jung doesn't discuss belief really.

SS: Belief is irrelevant there. I remember a conversation about this issue with Michael Fordham years ago, where he just simply said—I was asking what he thought about this—I met God once and didn't like it one bit! He was speaking of his own near death experience.

JH: But belief is captured in the realm of religion and Christianity makes a big deal of it. Credo. And the Christian God, you know, starts with the credo, I believe in Jesus Christ, and so on and so forth. That's part of the testament of faith. And I often wondered what would happen to the Gods of Christianity if no one believed in them. They require belief. If the God says you have to believe in me, then belief is what supports the God. The Greeks did not ask people to believe in their Gods. The Gods asked for certain rituals, or not to be forgotten, that was the most important thing. Not to be forgotten.

SS: Belief automatically valorizes disbelief. To say "believe in something" is a statement: the addressee is starting from a position of disbelief, or nonbelief, and is asked to move from that state to one of belief. This is the whole shift that Jung completely tries to discount. It's not a question of belief, nor was it a question of disbelief.

JH: Exactly.

SS: This belief/nonbelief pairing is what he tries to shift.

JH: Engagement. You engage with a phenomenon. Like the Greek Gods, you don't believe them, you don't believe *in* them.

They're myths. They belong to myth. Do you believe in myth? Do you believe that Hephaestus does this or that? Huge mistake. But modern man addresses questions in terms of belief or disbelief. Patriotism. You believe in the United States, you believe in the flag, whatever it is. That commits you and, by doing that, then your actions follow. That's all dealt with by philosophers. We don't need to discuss that. But Jung tries to, or he successfully does not bother with the question of belief and disbelief.

SS: That's the problem he's trying to get around. He says this is what is bedeviled.

JH: Yes, that's the credo, I believe. The creed. Why was it necessary in the history of Christianity to set up the creed like that? Even the Jews don't believe in the Ten Commandments. They carry them around with them, they set them up everywhere there's a tabernacle, but this idea of believing is very vicious.

SS: That's a tough one, we don't need to retrace theological history.

JH: Yes, we don't need it because, as you said, Jung doesn't deal with it. He's found his way through, or around, that.

SS: The question you can't ask is does Jung believe that his God is the son of the frogs? The question becomes completely absurd. He's had a particular experience that has come to him in a certain form.

JH: Or he believes in his experience.

SS: Does he believe in Abraxas? It's not a meaningful question. And it follows that he does not want to erect this into a creed, into something for others to believe in, which would be the next logical step, or a possible step, had he believed in his revelations.

JH: There's something else there. He doesn't go into the reality of the figures. In other words, how can you believe these figures are independent? How do I know they're not just part of me? How do I know that they're not complexes or projections of my various opinions? He doesn't deal with all of that psychologizing of what comes to him. He takes it as it comes. Isn't that partly what he means when he says he's an empiricist? Or what *I* think he means, that he's a phenomenologist, he takes phenomena as they come.

SS: That clearly is what he does in this text. I think that you start in 1914, when he writes the second layer. There he undergoes a cognitive shift, realizing that these figures are not simply personalistic in the way that we spoke about earlier, but that there is something collective about them. They're bound up with the event, either in a literal or in a symbolic dimension.

JH: The event meaning the historical event?

SS: The outbreak of war. The coincidence of his own imaginings with what is taking place within the world. In that regard layer two opens an experiment that is both hermeneutic and ontological. This was the most sophisticated hermeneutic reductionist. He could have reduced his fantasies back in the most intricate manner like anyone as he'd been doing for a decade, but he comes to the realization that precisely that mode of thinking had lost him his soul. So he had to throw it away. That mode of thinking had led to complete aridity.

JH: It's so great that he had the sense of soul to feel that he'd lost it.

SS: He had no option but to say, okay, let me see what comes in its own terms. As you say, a phenomenology, because everything else is thrown overboard in terms of his conceptualizing, but let's take it at its own terms.

JH: An extremely modern man.

SS: He does reformulate hermeneutics, he doesn't simply stay with the figures, but it's a completely different type of hermeneutic.

JH: He really was experiencing in himself, or with himself, a parallel to the world crisis, of the European war and the breakdown of the nineteenth century. He really was one of the great modern men of that period.

SS: That's the European avant-garde.

JH: Extraordinary. It happened in music, it happened in science, it happened in Vienna, it happened in painting, in architecture. He was of that crowd. He was on that Argo, he was one of the Argonauts.

SS: Something new had to be found because the highest values, as Nietzsche would have put it, had devalued themselves. They had led to ruin, to the battlefields of the Somme.

JH: You mention Nietzsche. Why was he so worried about Nietzsche? Why was Nietzsche a negative example? What was it, not Nietzsche's madness and so on, what was it particularly that Nietzsche did wrong that Jung didn't want to do the same?

SS: In the *Zarathustra* seminar there's a revealing passage where he says—this is the autumn of 1914—that the spirit had seized him and took him to a desert place, where he read *Zarathustra* for the second time. It was then that he understood the text.[113] So it was in the light of his own experience that he came to *his* understanding of *Zarathustra*. It was *Zarathustra* that he was grappling with, not the Nietzsche of *The Gay Science* or his other works.

JH: But he didn't want what he was going through to become Zarathustra's. He didn't want his *Red Book* to be *Zarathustra*. I'm making it very simple.

SS: Yes, there's the dialogue he has when he's with the librarian and the cook, where I think it's the librarian that interjects that Goethe and Nietzsche have written truer prayer books, as it were,[114] that these are an ersatz or a replacement of religion. Jung is not going with the Übermensch [superman].

JH: In other words, he was not going down the self-indulgent path.

SS: He was not going to overthrow Christianity. It becomes more extreme in that Nietzsche in his transvaluation is saying one has to just completely get rid of this Platonic Christian and Kantian structure, a complete overthrow, the "twilight of the idols." Jung's position is that one has to actually find one's way back to them, through recognizing their defaults, but revivifying them. In Jung's terms, *Zarathustra* would be a dismissal of the dead.

JH: Absolutely. It would have to be a new world.

SS: And a reinvention of the human. This is not what Jung is advocating.

SEVENTH CONVERSATION

SS: Let's begin with the sequence—procession—process issue. I've got a way into that.

JH: The idea comes from a sentence and you said you prefer to use the word "sequence" to the word "process."

SS: There's a very interesting movement from one to the other.

JH: In Jung?

SS: In Jung. What one finds initially in the *Black Books* is a series, a sequence of fantasies. What Jung then does in reflecting upon it is to suggest that underlying the multifarious figures, underlying the various fantasies, is a natural process of development. This is in his scholarly writings. For instance the red-haired maiden, Salome, Kali, these are all his soul. These are the anima. There's a process of condensation of the multiplicity of figures—

JH: Reduction?

SS: I say "condensation" because they're all combined into one, into what he calls at this time subject imagoes, which indicates how he shifts from the manifold expansion that characterizes his personal cosmology to the indication of a sequence of stages in the individuation process, with a few typical forms. First subject imago and, as he later calls them, archetypes.

JH: When does he do this?

SS: I think the critical text is *Relations Between the I and the Unconscious* in 1928.

JH: Volume seven. I have to understand that a little better, because one of the difficulties I have in general is with this word, the process of individuation, that it tends to be not only "process" of individuation but "progress" of individuation. It has a developmental impetus in it, I believe, in the way it's used, maybe just popularly, and I was wondering if that was in Jung, too, that the telos, for the sake of which it is driving, that there's a teleology in it in some way. When a group of things appear, one after another, they are not merely a sequence of things but are strung together like beads on a necklace. They have an order.

SS: That certainly is there in Jung. I'm reminded of a conversation noted by Ximena de Angulo in the 1950s discussing Ira Progoff's dissertation, and she raises the question to Jung as to his Aristotelianism.[115]

JH: Of *Jung's* Aristotelianism?

SS: Yes, entelechy. And it's clear from their discussion that she's hit a certain spot. People have emphasized far more Jung's Platonism and archetypal forms, but the connection between entelechy and individuation is this notion of teleology.

JH: And *process* tends to represent it. That word tends to represent it.

HILLMAN AND SHAMDASANI

SS: Jung is quite uneasy in this dialogue, when she has, as it were, put the finger on the question of crypto-Aristotelianism, you could call it.

JH: You see, I think you have to have goals. But he writes elsewhere that a goal is an ideal, not to be realized, and it's almost like a motivation but that's all it is. It sets up something for the impetus but not to be taken literally.

SS: There's actually an unpublished paper called "Images of the Goal" where he opens that up.[116] But that's at a later juncture, particularly in his alchemical reflections, where, as it were, the issue of the stone or the end point of the opus becomes figured in various ways that he then considers.

JH: Where is that paper?

SS: It's sitting in the archives.

JH: I gave a lecture at Eranos called something similar to that, "Images of the Goal." I think it was the last paper I gave there, and it's in my alchemy collection.[117] It's very interesting because there's a discussion about what a goal is. But I didn't want to get into that exactly. I wanted to get into the notion of sequence, because you used that word for what appears—this appears, then that appears, then that appears.

SS: What you find, say, in the *Black Books* is a sequence and in the handwritten manuscript, or one of the drafts of *Liber Secundus*, the chapters are simply called adventures. So "the next adventure."

JH: Great. That's a picaresque way of looking at things.

SS: There isn't a sense that it's necessarily all moving in one direction.

JH: In a literary sense, it's not a Bildungsroman, going toward the development of the character, but it's a picaresque, where this happens and then this happens and then this happens, and each event that happens is its own thing.

SS: But he does shift toward the other.

JH: Then something of the aesthetic gets lost. It's as if the aesthetic gets lost in the idea of meaning. The process gives meaning, puts it into the meaning of individuation. When it's in sequence, we are as if in a picture gallery, we've gone to a show, and we see this picture and that painting and this painting and they're all there in the room, and some are done earlier than others, and it's only if you look with the idea of development that you connect them. If you're looking at the idea of what each brings of its own, you're looking as the artist looks and as the critic looks, to see what each piece brings with it, the criteria of its own to be judged by and understood by. You don't put them all together unless you're doing a retrospective and then you see how the artist developed. But if you're looking at the paintings, it's each for itself, and that, to my mind, is the sequence and that's the way I like to look at dreams. I look at the phenomena and try to understand what they are. Sometimes there is a series of the same motif appearing three times in a row in several dreams, but even there one has to be careful to tie them into a meaning, a comprehensive meaning, stringing all the beads on one necklace, because each bead could go on a different necklace.

SS: The issue of process is there more in his attempt to translate the work to a medico-scientific public. It's there in *Relations*

Between the I and the Unconscious. It's not there within this work itself. Again, the operative term in the work is not "process" but "the way."

JH: The way? In the 1928 essays?

SS: No, in the *Red Book*. The critical term is not "individuation," which he could have used—he's already employed the term in print—but this is a work where he eschews that language.

JH: He's implying that there is a natural human urge to fulfill, that there's an entelechy in there, in our lives. And it disturbed him when that was clearly enunciated to him. Poor guy, it's a tough one!

SS: Caught red-handed as an Aristotelian!

JH: That's a tough question. But I think he depotentiated it in his discussion. I don't know the paper you're referring to, that's still in the drawer, but there are places in his writing where he says goals are to be taken only as signposts, goals are to be taken only as the impetus to make things happen, but never to be realized and so on.[118] So again the tension: he talks about them but then he is also aware of the dangers of taking them literally.

SS: Yes, I think that's a critical point.

JH: This should sober us all when we use the term "the process of individuation"—the individuation process, the symbols of the individuation process, or the stages of the individuation process. There's Esther Harding, Jolande Jacobi, the idea that you could learn the process and recognize it in your patients when the symbols appear.

SS: What you have in the *Red Book* is "the way," you have paths, you have streets. It's quite specific. "I'm on my way again."

JH: "I'm on my way again"? He says that?

SS: Yes, it's "way" with both a small "w" and with a big "w."

JH: If you're writing a book you can feel that. You're on your way, you're moving the chapter forward.

SS: If you look at the temporal sequence, *Liber Primus* and *Liber Secundus* unfold from October and November 1913 to February 1914. It's two-thirds of the work in that little time frame. This is not a massive period of time for a process of development. In this sense the process he is then speaking of is what unfolds, what takes place within him from 1913–14 to 1930.

JH: So the eruption, or the presentation of a sequence, that comes—

SS: —pretty much all at once, relatively speaking. What the process is is the attempt to shape it.

JH: To somehow find an underlying pattern, certain things that are connected, such as the idea of the anima.

SS: And to order it, to comprehend it, to integrate it and draw lessons from it. It's in a way a third-order reflection. I say third order because it's not simply the second layer of the text but it's his subsequent attempts to embody the lessons from it in life.

JH: But if you take each one of those figures, the redheaded woman, or whatever, and spend your time just with her for a while and let her speak and expose herself, and you expose yourself, so you go into that particular painting, what comes before and after it become secondary. That's more the *epoché* again, the phenomelogical bracketing out of any imposition on the phenomenon, but spending time with the phenomenon. Now, he does do that as well. It's what he does when he's in the midst of it. And my idea of therapy is to keep the patient in the midst of it, rather than labeling it as, for example, your anima is now showing you her red head.

SS: The question is then types of narrative formation, levels of connection.

JH: The connection between and among the figures and images.

SS: Jung is in a certain sense doing both. The cosmology continues to develop while he is attempting to condense it into a series of regularities and typical forms. He's pursuing it in different registers.

JH: But you personally make this remark, you prefer the word "sequence" to the word "process."

SS: For me, sequence implies something that is simply happening. What one has to look at here quite closely is the act of construction. The *end result* in Jung's psychology is the idea of process. Look at it from a more science-studies approach, such as the work of Bruno Latour—nature is not what one starts with, nature is the result of a particular construction.[119] What Jung arrives at in his theory is a notion of process. But what I'm interested in looking at is how he arrives at that. So you have to suspend naturalism. Also from a historical perspective you have to suspend any belief or disbelief in Jung's ideas and try to look at how he put them together.

JH: That means you have to suspend Jung to understand Jung. Again this is the idea of the historian as the therapist. You are interested in how he put it together, or what I call "seeing through" what's there to see "who" is doing "what" to it.

SS: What I see is a sequence of images, a sequence of dramatic dialogues, that by the time you reach *Relations Between the I and the Unconscious* becomes a process of development. Now simply to go back and read the book and say that there is a process of development—it took him fifteen years or so to arrive at that—doesn't give him insight into how he came to it. That's the particular thing that interests me.

JH: I see. What brought him to that mode of organizing. Now there was something else we thought we needed to touch on.

SS: There's a question of resistance to the book.

JH: Has there been resistance to the book from the outside, from critics, from newspaper articles, magazine reviews, and so on?

SS: At this point, the only hostility I've witnessed and encountered has been from a few people in the professional Jungian world.

JH: So then evidently the book is a threat either to them as professionals or to their ideas as theoreticians, or perhaps to their faith, to what they believe is Jungian, what they're practicing or living. We'd have to dissect some of that.

SS: I think the first level is that it challenges the whole notion that Jung is something known, dead and buried and been developed from. It's as if the man has crawled up from his grave, like an old wine that is still full of vigor.

JH: So he's one of the dead who is suddenly speaking.

SS: Right, and they don't like what he's saying. This is Jung one hundred percent proof. After the dilutions, after the mixed marriages with every flavor of therapy, other forms of thought, you suddenly get undiluted, one hundred percent Jung. It's something that has been welcomed by anyone who is genuinely still interested in Jung. But I've heard it said by others: Why do we need this, haven't we got enough Jung? Why is the book so big? Or that it looks too much like a Bible. Well, it seems to have escaped certain people's attention that Jung's work does have something to do with religion! In the sense of meaning in one's life, these are not incidental questions. It challenges professionalism, and there's been a great deal of what I call transcendental ventriloquism in which opinions have become attributed to Jung that are those of various authors. His work has been nearly completely mangled by ideologists.

JH: One of the big ones was that Jung's work needed filling out in terms of developmental psychology, since he doesn't actually have a developmental psychology.

SS: We're back to the issue of process.

JH: Yes, and he doesn't really have a theory of neurosis, so it had to be filled out with childhood in particular: that the family and childhood is what is missing in Jung. So this all had to be filled out and the school that filled it out best were the Kleinians and the Anna Freudians, the leaders of British thinking in psychotherapy. If that was your thinking, then this book pays no attention to it. No attention at all. It is the continuation of the notion that Jung neglected a critial aspect of life. Actually, he did plenty on children's dreams.[120]

SS: He actually spent more time observing children than Freud did. Freud is more interested in psychosexuality, infantile sexuality and how it's played out in adults' remembereance of childhood, rather than childhood per se, which interested Jung more.

JH: And the one big case of Freud's, which was that of "little Hans," was never Freud's patient. It was a patient of Freud's who was the father of the child. Freud saw little Hans I think once.[121] But this is an aside. You seem to think that the resistance is contained within the Jungian community, that the Jungian community is not representative of a wider resistance.

SS: To now, the broader public has lauded and welcomed the book.

JH: You have had no moments of people standing up and saying that this is wacky and what are we doing here with this strange book and so on and so forth.

SS: Only among Jungians. These are quite literally the only criticisms I have received—this book should never have been published. Also, the other aspect that it challenges is that people expected something like automatic writing or sex diaries or something that could be consigned as private in the conventional sense or a dream journal, in other words, something that could be safely seen as a prestage of what followed and you could simply say, okay, we have what is essential. This is also where there's a point of resistance.

JH: We have what is really worked out and these are prestages.

SS: We don't need to look at it. But then you suddenly see that this in fact shows Jung's personal cosmology and that it's not present in the published work and not reducible to it.

JH: And as you pointed out already, it's worked. It's years of work. Reworked and reworked.

SS: He spent more time on this than on anything else, any other work. This is a person who, in terms of his major books, wrote at a furious pace. This is a man who could crank out a six-hundred-page book in one big burst of creativity. This is not particularly long, but what is exceptional is the degree with which he struggled with it. The challenge then is to say hold on a minute, maybe the concepts aren't where it's at where Jung is concerned.

JH: I think there's something else involved. It's the idea that the person who really knows Jung is the person who has been through Jungian analysis. This idea comes to me from my life in Zurich. The people who are the spokespersons for Jungian psychology are analysts who have been through analysis of the Jungian variety and who practice it and study it and understand it from within patients and themselves—these are the authorities, these are the people. Therefore Jung himself said, back in 1916, that only those who had had fifty hours of analysis could be in the Psychological Club, if I remember aright. And that idea was taken up by the Clubs in New York and in San Francisco. The idea was that you had to have been analyzed in order to be able to understand Jung. Now, this book is presented by you and by a publisher and by Peck and several other people, but it's not presented by Jungian analysts, and they're the doges, they're the ones who understand Jung. Now, that pretension, or that hypothesis that they live with, I think, is what I believe gives the resistance. It means Jungian psychology belongs to analysts.

SS: Which is certainly not how Jung saw it. His prime focus was to form a science of psychology, a science of complex psychology, which only secondarily had applications in education and psychotherapy. Psychotherapy, as far as he was concerned, was not a science, so there's no point in trying to formularize it or to turn it into a method.

JH: This was one reason, when the institute was founded in '48, why he said the institute was a research center, with teaching of certain basic things such as anthropology and folklore. It was not a training institute.[122]

SS: No, he had no interest in that.

JH: And that was late in his life. But I think, I know, one of the difficulties that so-called archetypal psychology has is that, from the very beginning, it seemed to me it depotentiated the role of the analyst. It meant that the idea of the archetype could appear anywhere—it can appear in the movies, it can appear in painting, it can appear in the madhouse, it can appear in children. The archetypes are the universal, mythical forms. They appear everywhere. And one of the places they appear is in the clinic, in actual patient work. But that's only one out of a plethora of places. This relativizes the role of the analyst. The archetypal idea is a cultural phenomenon, and the practice of psychotherapy or analysis is only one place where you work with it. In terms of prestige, that lowers the place of the analyst.

SS: Quite clearly Jung sees himself, to use one of Nietzsche's expressions, as a physician of culture.

JH: He uses that term itself?

SS: Nietzsche uses that term.

JH: A physician of culture. I think that's very much what he was doing.

SS: Critically, what Jung comes to, during this period, is that the key issue of suffering is loss of meaning. Loss of meaning is not something purely individual but it's culturally determined, hence his intense preoccupation with historical issues. It's not that the individual has tripped up and gone astray in life in a purely idiosyncratic manner, but he or she is in a horizon where in Jung's understanding the traditions that should offer them sustenance, such as the churches, such as the academy, such as science in the true sense of the word, don't anymore, and it's then not surprising that an individual ends up in that predicament. So while Jung is attentive in his practice as a physician to the care of the individual, his main focus in his work is on getting to the root of what he considers these problems. And those roots are historical. And cultural. Thus his preferred collegiate network was the scholarly community at Eranos.[123]

JH: People who were also trying to move their fields.

SS: It was *not* other psychotherapists. It's not that Jung did not also engage with that network. He did. But that wasn't where he found collegiality. It wasn't where he found conversation that was mutually enriching.

JH: And many of those who were steadily at Eranos were also in a very peculiar position in their own fields. They also were adventurous, they also were an avant-garde in the field and were true scholars, but they were trying to reimagine their work. They were concerned with the loss, the fall, or what Corbin calls "the exile." The temple is broken. But the only trouble here with the resisters, or the only answer the resisters have, is that yes, that's true, physicians of the culture, but Jung tells us *how* the physician of the culture has to work. He has to go into analysis and go inside himself—not the physician but the patient. If we're going to restore the culture, we have to go in like a rainmaker and put ourselves in order and that's what a Jungian analyst does. He helps you put yourself in order.[124] Then you can come out and help the culture, and that was used again and again.

SS: That was Jung's commitment. That was his understanding.

JH: Okay, but then the analysts *do* have a priority, then their resistance is right because they're saying: we are doing Jung's work. We are trying to restore the culture, individually, one by one, by people, because Jung in that essay written late in his life called *The Undiscovered Self*—bad title, it meant something different in German, *Gegenwart und Zukunft*, *Present and Future*—the future hangs on the balance of each individual.[125] So the analyst who's able to work with the individual and bring that individual to a consciousness that Jung has opened the door to *is* the proper representative of Jungian psychology.

SS: But it's the individual only with respect to a situation where an individual grasps that his problems are superindividual. It's not the individual as a monad.

JH: Okay, it's not my personal development of working through my messes.

SS: That's not going to go anywhere. That's not going to have any broad input. It's the extent to which the individual problem coincides with a societal problem at large.

JH: It's a question of understanding the rainmaker. What the rainmaker does is connect with the cosmos. And that means the dead. The buried dead, the lost history, as well as the cosmos as the beauty of the world.

SS: And it's realizing what is of significance.

JH: I see what it is. We've taken the rainmaker as getting *himself* in order, and that *himself* is an entirely narrow personal structure.

SS: He's the one who makes it rain, so his self is of interest only to the extent to which he can constellate rainmaking powers. This is an interesting issue, I think, to highlight concerning Jung. His self-experimentation is also a therapeutic experimentation, in which he's interested in himself only inasmuch as there can be an outcome of significance.

JH: I wouldn't even say an outcome of significance, meaning rain, but also because he begins to realize he can't do anything at all about it himself.

SS: What is of concern to Jung, through his confrontation, is his experience, inasmuch as it coincides with something larger than himself. That's the point where his experience becomes significant from that perspective.

JH: And that would be already getting yourself in order?

SS: Yes, and there's a selectivity in that. There's a question of significance regarding this aspect of my experience. This is a bit where it intersects with something of collective importance.

JH: That's where it's cosmological.

SS: Yes, he's interested in his fantasies in 1914, primarily inasmuch as they intersect, coincide, with the zeitgeist, something outside of himself.

JH: And that's misread as his magical thinking. This is very important. That's misread as paranoid, delusional, magical thinking, megalomania. He thinks he's dreaming about the First World War, and that explains it all, whereas there's another dimension, which is his own personal life—why doesn't he realize his own complexes here instead of talking about Siegfried and all this stuff?

SS: Yes, this is an idiot who is in a paranoid defense.

JH: Exactly. A paranoid defense against self-understanding.

SS: In 1912 Jung is a master of reductive explanation. I don't think that would not have been the first thing he himself would have thought of.

JH: You said something significant there. The only thing that is important is if there *is* the connection with the zeitgeist, with the actual cosmos.

SS: Otherwise it becomes self-indulgent, it's not going anywhere. There's no wider relevance to it.

JH: You see, this would be one of the places where there's resistance, because if you're looking at it in terms of what analysis is supposed to do you're supposed to make yourself aware of your own shadow, your own projections, your own megalomania. And the moment you begin to talk about something parallel with what's going on in the world—just a parallel—you're in a defensive projection. Do you see?

SS: That's cutting off the bridges. That's cutting off the interconnections.

JH: Well, it's not following Jung, that's the main thing. It's taking the view of the pathological again. And not understanding the depth of the need of the human being in the cosmos. That's where my problem with modern psychotherapy is, that it is a clinic without a cosmos. The clinic works within the big bang theory, or the senseless world, or why get better?

SS: "Cosmos" is a big word. Who today has a cosmos? As we mentioned in terms of the ecology movement, how can one characterize what is a widely prevailing cosmos that is partly made up of pop science? This is a strange sort of cosmos. It is real, but it's fairly unstable.

JH: Jung had a cosmology, though.

SS: Jung did, but I'm saying that if one just turns to look at the situation in contemporary culture today . . .

JH: It's a pretty chaotic cosmos. It's pop. I don't want to do that. I'm getting excited and exhausted all at once, and it seems that what is offered by the *Red Book* is the opportunity for realizing that what goes on in myself, the rainmaker, only matters if it is connected to the rain. If it's just working out something, my marriage, my father, my children, whatever it's working out, that's not connecting me to the rain. And Jung offers the thought that it must be connected, and it puts the clinic into a cosmology.

SS: That's how I think he understood the rainmaker notion.

JH: That's satisfactory, because I've never liked the rainmaker notion. I've always thought this was a retreat, it was a way to keep people in analysis for years, so they could work on themselves and then one day they could reenter society.

SS: I see it as more of service than I've seen sometimes in some gurus in India, a notion of real service to the other, service to what is outside of themselves.

JH: Bhakti yoga, in a way.

SS: I've seen instances of that, levels of individual concentration and self-sacrifice, powers to effect change that are at the service of others, where it's not for self-improvement, and it does involve a level of self-effacement. For Jung, the rainmaker, as I see it, is not concentrating on himself for his own sake, for the sake of putting his own house in order, but it is concentrating on himself only inasmuch as he can constellate rainmaking powers. It's a degree of service. He's of significance only inasmuch as he can effect a certain change.

JH: He's in service to a much wider world.

SS: He's in service to the community. He considers himself as significant only in that dimension. Nietzsche said the teacher considers their experience as significant only inasmuch as it can inform their students.[126] Jung is using himself in that capacity. In the *Red Book*, he's turning himself over to others, he's making something of his experience, but only those elements he thinks have import to others. He is only significant in that regard.

JH: That's very helpful in regard to the rainmaker. It's not just putting yourself in order, in this very narrow sense of the self.

SS: The individual is a gateway; as I see it, the issue is not simply one of solving individual neuroses, individual suffering, but dealing with those aspects where the individual suffering intersects, coheres, is in direct connection with collective problems.

JH: And the biggest of all collective problems, as we've discussed, is the suppression of the dead. Not hearing the voices of history. Not hearing what we've lost. And the fear of the dead, the fear of death, in our culture.

SS: That's the theme of the *Red Book*, which is, "We need the coldness of death to see clearly."[127]

EIGHTH CONVERSATION

JH: I think people ought to be grateful for what you've put into it.

SS: It's been very interesting and stimulating for me, and it's made me think. I first read your work when I was about twenty-one or twenty-two, and at that point *Re-Visioning Psychology* was the first thing I read that showed a possibility of an engagement with Jung without being doctrinaire, in the sense of engagement with his ideas, and the spirit of his work, without necessarily subscribing to his particular ideas. It gave a possibility of staying with something as a field of concern, and so I moved away from psychology into the history of psychology, and in that regard it was your support and that of Michael Fordham that encouraged me to say, well, okay, maybe there is something in this. Thinking back over some of these points, at one level I think my engagement in the early days with your work has left its traces. It's formed part of what a phenomenologist might call a prereflexive consciousness.

JH: It's where one does the most damage to other people!

SS: It's there without my explicitly thinking about it.

JH: Part of the formation.

SS: It did mark the translation in certain points, such as the point we indicated earlier, daimon, a very specific choice, or the capitalization of "Gods," the avoidance of sneaking monotheism, as for instance happens in Hull's translations of the *Collected Works*. Or the issue of "the God," again an avoidance of instituting a hierarchy within the figures, simply through translation effects.

JH: Hull's vision of the world comes through his translation. Well, I'm glad to hear that. Small things that really matter.

SS: One is aware at that point of psychological and theological effects of editorial and translation decisions.

JH: Psychological effects of editorial decisions, yes.

SS: The main issue I had was deciding what the *Red Book* was, because what I found myself confronted with was a manuscript corpus: variant texts, no one of which was the same, running from the *Black Books*, to the *Calligraphic Version*, to the *Corrected Draft*, the *Handwritten Draft*—

JH: —how to make order, just simple order of this—

SS: —and even such a basic issue as paragraphing.

JH: And not knowing what comes first, what comes second?

SS: I established that in terms of the sequence. But with the paragraphing, you have the *Handwritten Draft*, where the sentence length is close to a prose poem, and at the other extreme one has the *Calligraphic Version*, where you have pages and pages without paragraph breaks. So it's a question of deciding the right unit, the semantic sequence. The ideal way to publish it would have been to publish five volumes. But I knew if I'd proposed that I would have been told to go and jump in the lake.

JH: You mean publish the *Red Book* in that way?

SS: Every single draft. A complete variorum. Which no publisher would have taken on. That remains a task for the future. What I then tried to do was to present one text—

JH: —and then make the notes—

SS: —and have the layering in the footnotes, so you could see the variations. Even then it was a fairly late decision to have footnotes instead of endnotes.

JH: You see, this is the historian's concern and the editor's concern, but you have an intimate knowledge of what Jung intends, more than anybody else could possibly have. We used to hear of the closeness Barbara Hannah and Marie-Louise von Franz had to Jung, and there were people earlier who would talk *for* Jung, but they were always loaded, it seemed to me, with what he did with them. That is, his angle. Let me explain what I mean. In the little play I wrote for the Fassnacht of 1954, Jung came with Emma Jung and we had a party. One of the skits was different people go to see Jung and they come back out and they say, Jung said I'm a sensation-type, Jung said I'm a so and so: he answered the same question for each person, he gave them what they came for. That seemed to me something that was going on when people went to see Jung. They came out with the Jung *they* wanted to see. Do you follow me? And I felt that this was going on in Zurich all the time, and I never knew what Jung really thought about this or that, because it would always be filtered by someone who had an angle, a card to play in the game. Now, talking with you, I don't know your cards, I don't feel you have them in the same way. Maybe it's because you're not a Jungian in the orthodox or card-carrying sense, maybe it's because you're a historian and you have a discipline of another sort. Whatever it is, that should give any reader, or anyone who listens to you, an opportunity to know something deeply. I don't want to say objectively because I don't know what that is, but deeply, through real deep familiarity.

SS: While I was engaged on this work, Jung felt to me like a cell mate in a prison.

JH: A soul mate in a prison?

SS: A *cell* mate.

JH: A cell mate or a soul mate!

SS: People have often asked me what I think about Jung or how I feel about him. That's an irrelevant question. I couldn't answer that because you just wake up and the guy's there. The task was one of tracking his thought, of thinking how he thought through something, and then the work was finished. While working on this, I'd often play a game with myself whenever I was working in his library in Kusnacht, which was one of taking down books and trying to guess which passages would be underlined or annotated. It was a question of checking one's nose, like a hunter after prey. Am I on the right track? Am I able to read these texts in the way that he's reading them? To catch sentences that would strike him.

JH: It takes tremendous patience, though. There's another word for objectivity, which I feel is much better, and that's "patience." It's not the same as obsession, because obsession can make you very narrow-minded. But patience means just patience. Suffering with it. And also being in the cloud of unknowing a lot.

SS: But it rewarded the work, because it's that which gave me the confidence to do the level of editing I needed to do, the level of editorial decision making, and it's like acclimatizing to a dark place. As an example, when I first encountered the text, it was so discrepant with the myths and fantasies of the work, starting from the garbled version of *Memories*, through to Laurens van der Post and biographies and so forth, that I just didn't know what on earth to make of it.[128]

JH: This is when the *Red Book* came out of the vault?

SS: Before that, when I found the first transcription, in 1996. One of the best decisions I made was to stop trying to understand it. I tried simply to start translating it, and to enter its world, such that Jung's figures became as familiar or if anything ultimately more familiar to me than my own. I was simply steeped in it.

JH: In that position, you're a pathologist. You're just seeing what's there, turning it over, the next bit, the next bit, or somebody who works with old papyrae.

SS: That's what Collingwood used to call the empathic imagination.[129] It was only when I felt fully steeped in it that I could then step out and contextualize it. I then felt I could move in and out of the world of his figures.

JH: The years in which you were doing not psychological understanding but your French Freudian work and your deconstruction reading. I remember going to a bookstore with you and your pointing out a whole series of books, and I bought some of them and I thought afterward, my God, when am I going to study all this? That gave you some kind of training, but what kind of training? It wasn't a diversion.

SS: To me history is practice, a means to get at questions of engagement, philosophical questions. History is a mode of gaining traction.

JH: Whereas you don't have that in those texts. They're presenting ideas.

SS: I felt at a certain point that contemporary philosophy was lacking grip, in that continental philosophy was becoming a form of self-referential literary criticism.

JH: I would say very self-referential.

SS: It has no purchase on what's taking place in the world, on politics. One would say, What does Heidegger have to say about that?

JH: Lots of new language, too, new terms.

SS: Also a degree of complexity, which in a way depotentiated the phenomena. I came to think that this complexity's already there in the world and the problems one is dealing with. The question is to describe it in the clearest manner. It seemed to me that these vast hermeneutic systems acted as if the world itself were impoverished and needing signification to be given to it.

JH: Yes, they were emptying the world.

SS: A vast depotentiation. I wanted to say, look, it's already full of significance, the question is how to read it.

JH: It is an interesting thing to move from that world into the depths of Jung. Very different.

SS: Yes, it's very different.

JH: But now we're at that place where the *Red Book* is out, it's published in many different languages. It'll appear in Chinese, no doubt. Psychology can't ignore it. The Jungians can't suppress it or resist it. Something about the human psyche will have to be reformulated and rethought, based on this epic opus.

SS: It gives Jungian psychology a chance to go to hell and recover its soul.

JH: That's good. Or aware that it's in hell, and lost its soul, that would be the job, because a great deal of what I read—and I don't read much any more of what's contemporary—but they're writing about the movies and they're writing about all kinds of things that are today's world, and they're with it, they have lots to say, many insights. There are three thousand official Jungians, something like that. So there is a world at work. But whether they—I say *they* but *we*—whether *we* can come back to being physicians of the culture, not interpreters of the culture. That's the point. You can write about the movies, and see Jungian psychology all over the place if you want, but that's not the job. Physicians of the culture—I call it therapy of ideas. When people ask me if I practice, I say no, I no longer practice. I practice what I call the therapy of ideas. I think we're sick from ideas.

SS: It's an intellectual pursuit, but it doesn't feed back into those domains in the form of an active engagement.

JH: Does it really help the movies? Does it really help the painters? Does it help the world to be able to show the movement of Jung's thought in these events of today?

SS: Clearly not. It would just provide satisfaction for those who feel that—

JH: Well, it's showing there's a deep undercurrent, there's an anima at work, there's a resistance to the idea of evil at work. They're very deep Jungian positions that are expressed in ways we hadn't realized, in the movies, in the novels. They're in the ecological questions. I'm trying to find a justification for the way Jungian psychology is used as an interpretive tool. I'm leaning over backwards!

SS: It seems to me that the practice of interpretation has a utility in a pragmatic context. I can understand that, in the therapeutic context, interpretations are offered to a client, as ways of moving things forward, and that has a utility. If one goes back and takes examples, it's not specific to Jungian psychology. I don't see what Freud's interpretation of *Gradiva* contributes to literature. In that instance, it's simply an imperialism, it's laying down a flag. It's expository and that's how Freud uses it. But I don't see a direct utility.

JH: I was trying truly to lean over backwards. I wish I *could* see the value. I've been so condemnatory. Now in my old age I feel I have to be a little more generous, or at least try to understand what these people are doing. Because there's so much of it being done. If this is psychology after the *Red Book*, it doesn't take its juice from the *Red Book*. Psychology after the *Red Book* has got to confirm some of the things that are in it, such as what Jung means by the religious instinct, what he means by annunciation, the sudden realizations that come or that what you've emphasized about what you're doing is not for yourself. You're not working on your own neurosis for yourself, for your own sake, and your whole vocabulary has to be brought under scrutiny. Self-individuation process, unconscious, *the* unconscious, ego—I mean just an enormous apparatus has to be brought under scrutiny.

SS: What you have is that this book is outselling the conceptual books. So it happens willy-nilly.

JH: So it is a physician of culture?

SS: It's also in that sense acting as a physician of Jungian psychology, simply through its effect on a broad readership. The book is affirming the value of taking one's individual experience, one's individual fantasies, seriously.

JH: And it's opening the door to the spontaneity of the imagination.

SS: Who knows where that will lead in the contemporary culture.

JH: Exactly.

SS: That's where the lead *will* come from, the broader reading public, and the question then for professionals is whether they can keep up with it and be open to what ensues.

JH: The imagination.

SS: Because it throws open the doors.

JH: And it provides a technique for encouraging and learning from imagination. It gives imagination a much more concrete life than just the romantic notion of imagination.

SS: From a historical angle, what it provides is that now you can begin to join the dots. Look at how Jung starts with certain theoretical positions, with his cultural education, with his own crisis, how this affects his fantasies, the figures of his imagination, and how he reflects upon this in attempting to elaborate it and then, secondly, to constitute a universal science. This is itself an absolutely unparalleled window into the psychology of creativity. I don't know of any other instance in the history of psychology where we can find these steps documented.

JH: That's very interesting. I wonder what William James would do were he to study the *Red Book*?

SS: That's a fascinating question.

JH: He would get it. He could respect these things. I think it would confirm things of his too.

SS: A new chapter in *The Varieties of Religious Experience*.[130]

III
New York

NINTH CONVERSATION

JH: We're in the midst of this enormous project, which is not only the *Red Book*, it's what Jung calls the lament of the dead. It's the history of humankind, which affects every single living person and is what psychology is. To wrap your mind around this is a challenge that seems to grow as I go on working with this, and reading the transcription of what we've done and the conversations we've had already it seems superhuman, his life seems superhuman and what he was engaged with, and what we're left with. So trying to build or think about a psychology now must start from something enormous too. Maybe that's very exaggerated but that's the only way I can think about it.

SS: A shift occurs immediately when you stop thinking of Jung's work in terms of the imperative to come to terms with the collective unconscious. If you shift from that language to the confrontation with the dead, accepting the lament of the dead, one's understanding changes dramatically in that one enters a world and the problems one takes up and is confronted with are not one's own.

JH: The problems one takes up are not one's own.

SS: And the issue then is how one adapts oneself, how one situates oneself, to these challenges. One is not dealing simply with an abstraction, the collective unconscious. One is dealing quite specifically with the dead of human history.

JH: Jung calls it the dead. I think that's the best word for what it is. It doesn't mean it's dead. Rather it means the whole burden that the human being's soul carries.

SS: It's a sense of what preexists one and it's also what one will end up joining. So it's not something that is completely set apart but it's realizing that one is a part of something.

JH: And what we call life is that brief time of being separated from it, or partly separated from it.

SS: Yes, it's an interruption from something else that one does not know. It's a mystery suspended between two mysteries. This touches on something quite central to what he's attempting to elaborate.

JH: Even what he was attempting to elaborate, and where we're left now with this book and his excursions into so many realms, certainly shifts what we consider to be psychology—that it is about me, and it's about things that happen to me, and things I can work out some way or another and go to therapy for. Now it's there before I even came into existence, and I have a part in this, but it's not my deep personal life at all. At least, I get that from the way you read deep subjectivity in Jung. The deepest subjectivity is not personal.

SS: One could say he's offering therapy for the dead.

JH: Therapy for the dead.

SS: I think people will look askance if you say that's what your practice is but it's not purely flippant.

JH: We have to be careful here that we don't mix up what is psychology from what is psychotherapy. From what I read in these pages, Jung was not primarily concerned with psychotherapy. He was a medical psychiatrist, and he had his patients, but he was interested in exploring the psyche and finding ways to make those explorations more transparent to his patients. But that is not what therapy has since become.

SS: It's not for nothing that in the 1920s and '30s Jung recommended that people had psychotherapy *before* they came to him, and that they needed a preparation that should be gotten elsewhere.

JH: Which then became called the "personal unconscious." You worked on your personal unconscious, your life history.

SS: Yes.

JH: There's another very big question here. If it's not psychotherapy as it was conceived beginning with Freud, your personal history, what kind of practice does it have? Has it a practice?

SS: I think it very much does have a practice. If you read the *Red Book*, Jung allows the figures to work on him. It's not he who works on the figures. He lets them instruct him. The relation shifts.

JH: And he wants to bring them out.

SS: He lets them do with him what they will. Now, this is not without struggle, this is not without resistance, this is not without objections, so it's not simply giving himself over. He maintains a skepticism and a sense of criticism in his act of engagement. But his opening gambit, if you will, is to say that maybe these figures can instruct me and maybe I can learn from them.[131]

JH: A very big point, that he could learn from them. These figures know things I do not know.

SS: And that is the gambit. To say let me suspend my knowingness. Let me set aside my science. Let me set aside what I take to be my psychology and see if I can learn something directly from these figures.

JH: Doesn't he also doubt the word "Jung" and the word "I"? At a certain point, he doesn't agree that the "I" is me, or that I am the figure who's talking as Jung. He has a peculiar level of understanding that all of us are fictions, in a way, or figures.

SS: A relativization of his own standpoint takes place, which is a critical development. Initially, it seems to me, it's a disorientating development because he's left then in the manifold and what he attempts to reestablish is the relation between the various figures. Who is what, how are they related, and what is the appropriate level of independence to take?

JH: Then comes the question of finding an overall concept that could embrace, for example, the many female figures, or the dark threatening figures. He's still in search of overriding concepts that could embrace more of the phenomena under headings. Make order.

TENTH CONVERSATION

JH: What I was hoping we could do is move away from Jung and the *Red Book* a bit and into some of these questions that were given to us, such as Christianity, practice built on images and literature, cosmology, because there's a certain repetition in what we're saying now. Is there something you want to bring particularly? What is it that grips us both?

SS: Why *is* one still concerned with psychology? For myself, the project of the blind leading the blind, human self-understanding by human means alone, in other words, without appeal to transcendence, is a fascinating project, regardless of whether it worked or not.

JH: That's very interesting. That's the basic humanistic vision. Can we understand ourselves without some metaphysics, something transcendent, some cosmology that puts us somewhere, gives us legitimacy? And you say that it's worthwhile, even if you don't know what you've achieved when you're doing it?

SS: It's a fascinating project.

JH: That's what you think psychology is then? The human understanding of the human without benefit of Gods, myths, Jesus Christ, anything else?

SS: It's interesting to see what happens when one attempts to start without some axiom, some transcendence, some warrant.

JH: I like that. This is also how Jung recommends starting an active imagination: anything that comes into the mind, however trivial, disgusting, vast. Every "nonstarter" is a potential starting image, feeling, or idea.

SS: This would be expanding his methodological principle here.

JH: It doesn't matter whether it's a good idea or not, or anything, let's just see what happens if you have this adventure. Can a human being understand himself? Can he make a psychology?

SS: If you then look back from a historical angle, surveying psychologies of the twentieth century, you find yourself as in a Borges short story and see this plethora of imaginary worlds, a multiplicity of conceptions of the human being, so let's see how they work. It doesn't matter if they're true or not, these themselves are remarkable inventions, remarkable creations. They've taken great ingenuity.

JH: These would be more than folk psychologies. Just popular beliefs in something or other.

SS: Yes, but as we touched on, they all in the end become some sort of folk psychology. "Folk psychology" is not a terribly good phrase but I don't know how else to refer to the nonprofessional forms of self-understanding that give rise to different forms of human self-consciousness.

JH: You could say that we are generally today so unconscious of the form we're using for self-understanding that we don't realize we use strange systems of the brain, of sociology, of economic structures, all kinds of systems, for giving an account to ourselves as to why things are or why we are as we are. I think that's one of the major areas of unconsciousness.

SS: It's actually to be reflective about what one uses to understand oneself and others in various situations that one has picked up along the way. The question then, one would say, from an anthropological perspective, is not so much to study psychology as in a theoretical form, but to study how people explain themselves and explain others and what are the implicit forms of understanding they utilize. And this goes back to the question you posed regarding literature.

JH: If you include Borges in there and all the other extraordinary fantasy writers, and the understanding of the story of the narratives, which is supposed to say who we are or tell tales of us, the richness is enormous. So Jung's program of the collective unconscious, the archetypes, the figures, big as it is, seems rather unimaginative in the view of, say, Borges. The possibilities are limited. So the dead become again more and more important, because they would bring in something unknown or ungraspable or ultimately puzzling.

SS: To take up what you said about limiting, I think that it is inherently their function to contain the chaos. There was an article by Catherine Elgin and Nelson Goodman that I liked a lot on the epistemological value of stupidity, and their main thesis was that when one has differentiated knowledge, one has difficulty making a decision or choice. One can go astray more with a differentiated system, and there's a functional value in having simple categories. It's operational in various contexts, and it's simplifying.[132]

JH: So you want something that produces limitations?

SS: Limitations makes life easier to handle in various ways. If your question is simply whether a wine is red or white it's a simple situation, but if you're judging vintages, growers, particularly in Burgundy, getting it right is an awful lot more difficult. One sees that operational aspect, for instance, in regard to Jung's work, most clearly in connection with the use of typology. It's precisely its brutal simplicity that seems to make it so attractive for people. Suddenly the multiplicity of individuals is reducible to a set of easily compartmentalized types, and with that one thinks one knows how to relate to an individual. It gives one clues, indications, directions. I use that as an example.

JH: That's also stupidity.

SS: If you like, but it's useful. It makes certain situations navigable.

JH: Yes, but you know underneath that this isn't the way things are. If you have any intuition or sense of the way things are, you know they don't fit this schema.

SS: That then is another task, which interests me, becoming reflexive with one's categories, and unlearning one's categories, to try and be more responsive to what is there.

JH: Exactly. What are *you* bringing to it? Now, they tried to do that with the types. They say well, you see, you're looking at it all through the thinking function, and because you are that's the only thing you are seeing and you're missing this and this and this. So they *do* try to limit the categories but what is it that doesn't work? I don't think we want to go into a critique of the types. Jung says it's not for judging people, it's simply for working through ideas. Maybe this doesn't really belong. Back to your idea of limitation.

With the richness in this book, and all that you've discovered through footnoting and going back through personal papers and so on, where's the limitation? Is there limitation in what Jung's doing here? Isn't it just endlessly enriching and expansive and allowing everything, including the devil as part of Jesus Christ, the ultimate nonlimitation?

SS: There is a moment when he lets the chaos in. He says at one point, this was the night on which all the dams broke and he lets it in, but he doesn't remain there, within the anarchy, within the chaos.[133]

JH: And that's what you're saying he doesn't accept in Picasso and in Joyce, that they *do* remain in the chaos. Joyce's Nighttown.

SS: That is right. He attempts to discern its order.

JH: Assuming it has an order.

SS: At one point he says, "It is not formless."[134]

JH: "It is not formless." The dead have content. They have something to say.

SS: And they are related to one another. One can discern genealogies. He then also attempts critically to channel it, to bring something up from this into the day world, so the aspect of return becomes quite critical to him.

JH: We take that up and you must bring back, as he says in 1916, something of value when you return, otherwise it's self-indulgent.[135] Anybody can have weird, extraordinary experiences, talking to all kinds of Gods and figures, but unless something comes of this, unless you bring back something, it doesn't make you any better. You can't judge the value of the voice, you can't discriminate your voice from the voice speaking to you, and you have to. You have to know that's not you, with all this high-blown wisdom. But you have to listen to it. Now these are the messages we get from the book, and we know this, but what does it teach us about what more we can do, so that psychology follows this adventure into the human being, as you say, devising a mode for understanding ourselves and others.

SS: It's for understanding one's place in the world.

JH: You see, I think a cosmology does that. I don't think psychology necessarily does. Psychology may give you modes of understanding and you think you're understanding yourself and others. But if you want to understand the world, you have to have a cosmology, you have to have a sense that things fit, that they belong, that there's a need, a place to be given to it, and that there's more and more to grasp. It's the cosmos, and the Greek cosmos was an ordered and aesthetic realm. That's where we get the term "cosmetics." The realm of order, and the realm of cosmetics, beauty. Today the word is connected to women's decorations and jewelry. You have to have that or what the hell's going on out there? Why pay any attention to it at all? You have to have a sense that maybe you're here not to understand anything but to appreciate what's here. That's a cosmology, I think. In other words, living with the beauty of the world. I think that's what the Greeks saw.

SS: But aren't we in a context where people have outsourced cosmology? Someone else is sorting that out. I take it from the physicists, or the geneticists, or the biologists, or the neuro-scientists . . .

JH: I see what you mean, yes. The biologists and the brain people can give us a cosmology.

SS: Someone else is going to tell me about it.

JH: Yes, they can reproduce it.

SS: Within that sense, do people take on the task of forming a cosmology? Jung certainly does. He doesn't shirk that.

JH: Part of his cosmology is the continuing, living power of the dead. Would you say that?

SS: That's pivotal. In his view, we have to find a place for the dead in order to enable our own living.

ELEVENTH CONVERSATION

SS: The question we're revolving around is the lament of the dead. Who are the dead? What is so radical in this text is there's a shift in the hierarchy between the dead and the living. The questions of the living, the problems of the living, the suffering of the living can be answered, or addressed, only through attending to the dead. So there's a reversal of terms. Unless you manage to situate yourself with regard to the dead, you can't find a solution to your own living. What do you think about this?

JH: We're a very strange culture, our modern, secular Western culture, in which our conversation, yours and mine, is set. We don't have any ancestor worship, we don't have any true cult of the dead. Different pieces of the culture do pieces of things, but even the use of the phrase "the dead" is hounded with frightening things—it belongs on the other side. There's a radical separation in our modern culture between the living and the dead. All the medical work is life against death, to hold off death and prolong life, and at the expense of death, I would say. So when we talk about the lament of the dead, or anything to do with the dead, we have to realize where we are situated, with its deep, historical prejudices against what has been and what is buried, and what we have done to create a realm of the dead, because it's not merely those who went before us and died. It's all the depository of the accumulation of human psychic history, the history of the soul. Somehow, since Jung talks about a lament of the dead, they must feel or have felt abused or neglected or something. The first step would be listening to them, which he did in the *Seven Sermons* of

1916, this sort of inspired religious document. But what *is* their lament?

SS: I think prior to that is the notion that they exist. Following what you were saying, contemporary culture has in a way killed off the dead. It's a rather bizarre paradox. The first task that Jung finds himself confronted with is reanimating the dead, acknowledging that their presences exist and haunt us. Acknowledging that the dead *are*, and they have presences, they have effects. We turn our eyes away from future-orientated living and to what has gone before, in the shape of animated history, history that is not simply a record but history that is active.

JH: A history of living beings, who are all about us.

SS: The question is how does one hear that? Jung does it through his fantasy. In his view, fantasy is the portal to the dead that are still speaking within us.

JH: That's why listening to the fantasies, why the fantasies come from elsewhere, they're not the result of things we saw during the day, gives them an autonomous validity. So in a way what you're saying is that acknowledging their existence is already listening to the dead.

SS: That's the very first step, acknowledging there is no place for the dead.

JH: Would you tie the death of the dead to Christ's activity in the underworld and the insistence that there is only Christ's voice because he harrowed Hell and so on?

SS: It's an interesting connection. Christ has preached to the dead, he attempted to save the dead. Now in Jung's formulation the dead aren't satisfied. The dead that he encounters are restless dead, their questions are unanswered. In that sense the "harrowing of Hell," one could imagine, could be conceived of as a means of closing off the realm of the dead. They've now been dealt with.

JH: Vanitas, "where is thy victory," and so on.

SS: They've heard the Gospel.

JH: It's a very big question and I don't know enough text to understand the relation of Christ with the dead. I'm suspicious about what he said to the dead, and I don't know what his preaching was. I suspect it was somehow to depotentiate them, so there's only the redeemer's voice.

SS: I take it that the dead were Jews and pagans. They had not died in Christ.

JH: They were probably mainly pagans to begin with. They had not died in Christ, no. Do you know by chance what his preaching was? Does Jung talk about the actual preaching?

SS: What Jung says is, "No one knows what happened during the three days Christ was in Hell. I have experienced it."[136] He's undergone it.

JH: So in my daily life, listening to the dead would have something to do with being aware of the presence of all that's been, and as you say reorientating my look from a forward future to what have I missed, what have I let go of, what haunts?

It's not even that clear. It's really a sense that the living, as Eliot says, are only partly living.[137] You begin to feel, or even see, through the flesh, and things aren't as real as they seem. You're not as real as you seem. The things you think are real are not as you believe they are or want them to be. That seems to be the effect of the dead, the disengagement from what has seemed so vital and important.

SS: There's a striking expression that Jung uses after his heart attack and his death experience. He says he's come to realize that life itself is a prejudice, a working hypothesis, but not existence itself.[138]

JH: That's very good. I think that's what I mean, very much that.

SS: And he comes to the view that one has to conceive of one's life both in response to the dead and in terms of one's own becoming dead, so there is a sense of suspension as between two mysteries, which relativizes one's own existence. The weight that one places on one's own life, one's imminent concerns, shifts in both directions. It shifts both in terms of what has preceded one, which has gone on for aeons, and also in what one will become, and in that sense the legacy one is building up as far as what one is leaving to others. It becomes a kind of working space suspended between a larger continuity.

JH: It's almost as if you have to spend your whole life disengaging from your life, disengaging from the supposed reality of your living. I think that's what Spinoza and Socrates meant about life is the study of dying, that you leave these convictions of certitude about the whole business. I certainly feel lots of that now, whereas my friend Higuchi says he's living in the afterlife. Beautiful idea.

Meaning his life is over, he's living *after* life, but it's also the afterlife.

SS: Also, if I understand it right, we end being committed to life in a different sense. We're committed to what is present but accepting its transience.

JH: Transience. It's much more autonomous and inconsistent, I think. You really don't know the next day how you're going to wake up in the morning, or anything about it. Nothing. Or *if*. There's a huge freedom also. I'm thinking what it is about Jung's work that still grabs me, since it changed through the years, is a huge freedom in his work. Nothing means what you think it does. Everything's cut loose in a strange way. That sentence you quoted a minute or two ago—the difference between existence and living—that's a huge idea. Your daily living, to which you're devoted, is not the real thing. So how do you devote yourself to the real thing? And why? What's wrong with just living as it happens?

SS: I understand that at a certain point he came to see a larger perspective but it didn't pull him away from life. It actually gave him a deeper appreciation of life, because it sets it within a perspective.

JH: But "the larger perspective" is a phrase that doesn't go far enough in specifying that change. Certain things seem no longer to matter, and other things seem to matter intensely, and that question of value, or what Whitehead calls importance, as a basic category of life or existence seems very, very important. Important seems very important.[139] We live in a society where importance could be said to be totally screwed up, where it's given. For example, just one example, to go back to the idea of cosmos as beauty. If we think that the cosmos is an ordered system of some kind, the universe, with the way the planets move and a cosmology of that sort, then reason is the important way of entering the world. But if that's not important, if being moved, touched, if one's soul is encountered, if questions of love and death and beauty are what move the soul, then it doesn't matter how it all fits together, whether Einstein was right or wrong.

SS: But that's to conceive of the cosmos in a classical sense, in terms of order. But what if the accent, which I think it is more with Jung, is not on order but on what one could call fittingness?

JH: That's a very good word. It's the correct word.

SS: That things fit. That they're appropriate. It doesn't necessarily mean that there is a rational order. In fact, part of the experience of fittingness is precisely the sense that the order escapes one.

JH: And it becomes more *individual* fittings, rather than an overall.

SS: And appropriateness, in other words, in the sense that there is—

JH: Appropriateness, that's also part of the word "cosmos."

SS: There is an experience of mystery, where something feels right but one does not encapsulate it.

JH: This involves the arts very much. The right word, the right color, the right stroke, the right sound.

SS: One is given, in terms of articulation, fitting expression, to what is, or what one has encountered, what one has experienced.

JH: That's the response you say, a fitting response?

SS: I'm reminded of a statement by the painter Wols I once had up on my wall in my student days. It simply said: "Do not interpret music, do not interpret dreams, one must know that everything rhymes."[140] The sense that things fit together. Don't try to figure it out because you will lose it in so doing.

JH: That's your main objection to what you call the "guard rails" of the whole development of Jung's other side, where he tried so hard to find accommodation with the scientific worldview by devising concepts that were as close to the experience as possible. And that became Jungian psychology.

SS: In the text of the *Red Book* you find Jung actually setting aside the guide rails, setting aside his own psychology that he'd developed up to then, seeing to what extent he could let the chaos in without apotropaic magic. It's clear in his subsequent statements that this was what he conceived of as the crux of one's encounter with one's own depths, that this is what he saw as the essence of his therapy, his practice, which was to enable an individual to encounter his or her own depths.

JH: In individual symbol formation, as he called it. But besides those abstract words, encounter his own depths. That's crucial. And also that would mean encountering the lament of the dead, or at least meeting the dead in some way, recognizing the dead.

SS: To finding their *own* dead. Recognizing their ancestors.

JH: Now, our finding our own dead in the United States involves so much history, close history, one hundred and fifty years of history, slavery, civil war, brutalities of all sorts, Chinese oppression, it's just so huge, all the deaths of the Indians, and animals, that we're blocked in a strange way by personal guilt. We enter the realm of the dead overloaded to begin with, with Protestantism and guilt, so I don't know if we get to what you call ancestors. I don't know if we have a sensitivity to whatever that means.

SS: If we think of what we witnessed this morning, with Obama's motorcade passing right under our window to go to ground zero, and to see the speculation in the newspaper, the commentaries on what is he doing, what is the occasion?[141] One can conceive it precisely in the sense of appropriation to the dead. He's going to the shrine of the present day, to mark the significance of an event. That he has in some sense answered their lament, or recognized it and has not forgotten them. And that rejoicing in the culture in New York, the sense that the dead have not been forgotten, I find tremendously striking, coming from London. So I don't think it's lost, I think it's simply that its location has shifted.

JH: What he's doing by only talking to families and firemen and policemen, but not the public, and what he's doing by simply coming back to New York in honor of this event, already gives an answer to the lament of a certain sort. They're not forgotten, as you said.

SS: They're not forgotten, and in this instance vengeance has taken place.

JH: He's not doing vengeance.

SS: I think the act was one of vengeance.

JH: You mean the bonding?

SS: No, the killing of Osama. There's a Greek form, something out of Aeschylus. The dead have been avenged. The dead can now rest.

JH: Some of these family members have actually used those terms. That's an interesting thought. But it was a ritual vengeance in some way. I didn't feel it had the personal quality that George Bush had in the very first weeks. "We'll catch you wherever you are, you can't hide from us." This strikes me as more of a necessary closure, and in that sense ritual.

SS: It struck me as respectful the way he said nothing. There was no broadcast. He said nothing publicly but was seen to make his way to pay respect.

JH: And yet the decision, which was a huge decision, he took, and it had to be him that took it.

That was a curious diversion. I think it's very important because we're still playing out these roles, what you call Aeschylus' roles, that certain things have to be brought to justice. But when I hear the word "justice" used by announcers, I feel it as very different justice, that they were using it in a much more superficial way. When it's used in the Greek sense it means order is reestablished. Things have been impossible ever since and now they can be balanced.

SS: Something has been restored.

JH: Politically I don't think Osama's disappearance is going to make much difference, because I think he was, so to speak, "old hat" by now. But the idea of justice is not old hat, the classical idea.

SS: There's the idea in Jung that his psychology is not just for the living, it's for the dead. It's no accident that the *Sermons* in 1916 are teaching instructions to the dead. This is what the dead require. And he says quite explicitly at a number of junctures that his psychology, his work, was an attempt to answer the unresolved questions of the dead. The questions that were posed to him and that he took up.

JH: Does this in a way bear on your own work, your own calling in this work? Why are you doing it? If you can answer why.

SS: What I find is that the work doesn't leave me alone. And it doesn't matter at all that my own way of thinking is different. I find myself more sympathetic to the frame of mind of William James than to Jung, but James doesn't pose questions to me that make me think or that I have to figure out. There's a way in which I never feel that I've got to the end of Jung. There's something inexhaustible about him.

JH: Yes, that's right.

SS: It's like peeling an onion. Under a layer there's another layer, other questions emerge.

JH: That's what is so disappointing, so often, by his attempts to resolve his own richness with simplifications. For me, the law of opposites, or the idea of the self, is so disappointing. And I wonder if—although now we're going off track—he himself was disappointed with his own formulations.

SS: I wouldn't say disappointed. I would say he saw them as just that. Theory making was one of his activities, one of the things he liked doing. He found it satisfying. But he didn't mistake the map for the terrain.

JH: Good point. But that was just a little parenthesis. Before that, I had asked you, and was asking myself, What am I doing it for? What's got me?

SS: The question that I've had is can one ever know, can one discern the *ratio* of one's own activity. I've had more of a sense that the meaning of one's own activity escapes one, and necessarily so.

JH: That's good. But there are certain repetitions that happen in one's own activity that reveal its essence or its importance. I know that several times after an Eranos lecture, I felt I was only doing this for the dead. I was not talking to the audience. Twice, at least, I felt that. It was not for them. So it didn't matter to me if anyone understood what the hell I was trying to do.

SS: I felt that very much in editing the *Red Book*. I wasn't doing it for a contemporary audience. I didn't care if it sold or not or disappeared without a trace. I found myself in a situation that felt bizarre. It was unbidden, it was unchosen, where I had to sort out this manuscript corpus. I had to take up one of Jung's incomplete tasks. He left it unfinished, and he knew he'd left it unfinished. I was the poor sod who got dealt that one. The task was also unfinished by Cary Baynes to persuade Jung to publish it and set in within the context of his life, so those were the two people

I felt I was addressing. There was a sense also that I'd spent an absurd amount of time doing this.

JH: My life! I've spent my life on this.

SS: Yes, I could have written three books in the course of time that I'd spent on this. But at a certain point, when the expenditure has become so great, there is no option but to carry on, and simply to say, look, this has to be without calculation, without calibration, because I'm not the one to know the reasons.

JH: Now, was there another aspect to it, which was to keep a tradition alive? That was important for me, and still is. One of the reasons I like to put scholarly footnotes, which seem almost irrelevant, is that I know if I don't bring this in right here, no one will ever remember it or pay attention to it. It's the only way to keep the dead. For me the dead are very often what's gone before in the field, and these dead are remembered, because I've remembered to bring them back and show what they did. Fechner's only a little example, but many, many others. Why did I need to do that? Was this paying a debt to the dead? It wasn't to reestablish my scholarly authority because I don't have that much scholarly authority. I don't have a degree in Classics, just a lot of papers that are marginally within the field, and they're nearly all my own invention. So what was the reason? It was to keep a whole world from being lost. That's what *Freud's Own Cookbook* was about.[142] I knew nobody would remember any of these early figures in psychiatry unless they were a joke, unless they were some kind of parody, and only then would they be remembered, if at all. And it was a huge field that would be forgotten. No one cares about Griesinger . . . you know what I mean.

SS: That goes in a way to the heart of Jung's own scholarly activity. I counted that *Mysterium Coniunctionis* has around 2,300 footnotes, including at times untranslated Greek and Latin.

JH: That's another point. Just the erudition. There's supposed to be a remark by Foucault in which he said the only way to get out of the box of contemporary thinking, meaning sociological reduction, economic reduction, political reduction, all the systems we have for understanding what's going on, Freudian reduction, is to move up to erudition or move down to the indigenous. Great idea, brilliant. I thought about that a lot recently. I spent a lot of time making those moves. My move toward the Greeks was for erudition, it wasn't for religion, although it had a little side aggression in it to get rid of the Christians by going through the Greeks. I'm not taking on the Jews directly, that was too much, I couldn't handle that. If I'm going to deal with the Christians, I can't meet them as a Jew, I couldn't handle it. But maybe as a Greek I could meet them, as a Romantic, that kind of Greek. Erudition. And Jung and Freud, although Freud used it very differently, were never afraid of that.

SS: Another level to that, which is one reason I find it vital as a historian, is the sense that one reads, say, certain texts in the nineteenth century, such as nineteenth-century psychology, and realizes these were the brightest minds of their age. They're dealing with questions that we haven't resolved now. So this makes one think there is no natural selection in ideas. There is no sense that we are left simply with the ideas that prevail because they were more fit for life, or proved in any way their inherent superiority. In many ways one finds the opposite has happened. In psychology one had the triumph of Freud, one had the triumph of Skinner. One didn't have a school of William James, or one of my heroes, Joseph Delboeuf.[143] It enables one to see the contingency in the present and to relativize the present. It also enables one to envisage new possibilities—one has shaken off, one has desolidifed the given. So erudition is not purely scholastic.

JH: No, but it is part of the dead. When you realize how erudite some of these people were, and not just in the nineteenth century, wow. That's what's missing, you see, there isn't that love for thinking in the contemporary Jungians. I don't even know which among his first early circle had that love of learning.

SS: Not many. But I'd like to return to this issue of erudition. The other significant level, as I see it, is it takes one outside of oneself. Problems that people encounter in their immediacy, one finds, are issues that some of the finest thinkers have been concerned with for centuries. They're not necessarily anything new. One manages to move from the constriction in the present to a wider horizon, which itself can offer new perspectives.

JH: It's not only a wider horizon, there's something less known about it, because it's elsewhere or farther away, and it releases more imagination, the erudition does. There are stranger things in it, just as with the indigenous, and it prompts the creative imagination in the scholar or in the worker. That's lost if you don't go in those two directions.

TWELFTH CONVERSATION

SS: One of the things we touched upon was the significance of literature for psychology. What do you see that literature can offer to psychology?

JH: My goodness, that goes right to the present heart of my interests. I feel that our way of understanding people in the practice of therapy is terribly inadequate, and we have our case studies and we have our diagnostic manuals, which have hundreds of categories of diagnoses, and we never get the feeling of a living person. Whereas in the nineteenth century, and even into the twentieth, the case histories were written up in such a way that you saw the handwriting of the patient, you saw all kinds of details from his or her work life, you saw reports of the patient's children—everything was condensed into these case write-ups that were very vivid and sensuous. There was a kind of imaginary or literary figure there in the descriptions. Now, I can see why the statistical reports that you get in the diagnostic and statistical manual state that so many people who get this kind of schizophrenia will collapse after so and so many years into this kind of et cetera, et cetera. There's an enormous amount of what's called evidence-based reports on prognosis and treatment and so on. It's very, very much psychiatric and medical. Now, if the basic figures who determine a human life are not mine to begin with, but are these figures that Jung encountered, hundreds of patients have encountered them in likewise fashion, so why not begin there for getting models or images for what is a human life? What is a human soul made of?

Before there was psychology around 1900, in a case history sense, we had novels. All through the nineteenth century Jane Austen, Tolstoy, Turgenev, Balzac wrote the most extraordinary descriptions of human lives and their tragedies, their sufferings, their humor, their peculiarities, their hungers, their bestialities, their perversions—*everything* was in the literature. And an ordinary person read lots and lots of literature, or followed someone such as Dickens around on his lecture tours, just to pick up these narratives and learn about how it is. Now it seems to me the interwovenness between the figures per se, in themselves, is part of the job of learning, the practice of the image, seeing how they work with each other, what they build, how they influence. That's exactly what literature was doing, *has* been doing. It's become more sophisticated in many ways. But the narratives about people's lives, telling people how this woman so often collapsed when anything went wrong in the family, took to her couch, took to her bed, or fainted, or the story of the man who was always the dramatic lover boy of the neighborhood, well, novels were filled with this descriptive, rich material of the way human lives are filled with hypocrisy, deception, petty cruelties, denials, blindness, everything you can think of. It seems to me that the way back to understanding human nature is through returning to literary studies, not scientific case descriptions, or statistical analyses, or whatever else is being taught in the classroom for the therapist. It would be a study of life through good writing.

SS: I see where you're going with that, but I think there's something potentially problematic in the status that gives to literature, and in the way that it can be understood, so I'd rather look for a more neutral language. What I see as significant there is the function you see literature as providing. I would describe it as providing rich articulations of experience.

JH: Very good.

SS: In which individuals can recognize themselves and others. Now people can find that in many sources, it's not just in literature . . .

JH: In drama and so on.

SS: Also paradoxically in the failure of psychology's will to science, it gets turned to as another means to provide articulations of experience. It becomes read as literature. It's not for nothing that with the demise of psychoanalysis the last retreat of psychoanalysis has been to the literary departments.

JH: That's right. Its last bastion.

SS: Personally I am wary about evaluation. I'm more interested in looking at how people use various things. So in that sense psychologies are used as vehicles for the articulation of experience, through which individuals recognize themselves and recognize others, and they find psychologies to their taste. I have a certain wariness of valorizing one form of articulation of experience over others.

JH: I guess I should use the word "story" rather than literature. But it doesn't matter. What I'm really after is what you call the rich articulation of experience, so that one sees something that offers insight.

SS: "Insight" is the critical term, because the psychologies that have been successful have been precisely those that have to my mind provided simple means of being operationalized. They've become psychologies that are adept at the micromanagement of human relations, and can be put to work regarding how to do things to other people, not necessarily to provide differentiated insights. It's precisely their simplicity that accounts for their comparative success.

JH: We probably should go back to this question of literature again. Anyway, it interests me a lot. And I'm using literature in a very wide sense because I mean the arts, including the great dramas, the Greek dramas, especially, and Homer and Shakespeare and so on. The proper training for the practical therapist who has to understand human nature, and make something of human lives, remains with Natasha in Tolstoy's *War and Peace*, with Falstaff in Shakespeare: these are living figures that remain more that any human being you may ever have met. When I say they remain, I mean they are psychic realities, and more can be learned from what you call the more careful, or more brilliant, or more articulate of writers than by studying case histories. There's very little you learn from a case history that extends into other people, into life, into lessons learned. So that's part of it. The proper study for the therapist is reading lives that are not human lives but are the deepest part of human life, that is, the powers that live us and are articulated so well by good writers. But not only good writers, that's what's curious. There's a second part to this, which is that psychology itself should be based not on statistics and sociology, whatever we want to call it, political realities and so on, but based on the story that a human life lives and is presented by literature. How did we know psychology before there was any? People read in the nineteenth century, especially women, and also wrote extraordinary novels, short stories, and there was a kind of deep learning about how we are, how the human psyche works, from the reading of pop novels, but also reading the great tragedies, how the Gods intervene in our lives, and that seems to me the aesthetic basis of our study, of our work, and it's been completely on a wrong track. Since that discussion about beauty in Joyce and Picasso, we still have a hunk left over there, which is that something hasn't been dealt with properly by Jung or the Jungians regarding the primary importance of beauty and therefore aesthetics for the life of the psyche.

SS: If one looks at those questions in Jung's own practice, in regard to the *Red Book*, one sees here a situation where what he eschews is conceptual language. At that point he realizes conceptual language is inadequate to encapsulate the language of the soul. It is the language of the soul, as far as he's concerned, because it is his dialogue to and with his soul. A new language is needed. It's a literary language but it's not a fictional language, he's quite adamant on this point. It is all *Wahrheit* [truth] and not *Dichtung* [poetry], as he says to Cary Baynes,[144] and he struggles with this. He has to use a language that conveys, that evokes the emotional power of the experiences in question.

JH: That's the big thing. The language of psychology today doesn't convey any emotion or any beauty of the experience itself that it's describing.

SS: That is the main difference between the language of evocation, as I understand it, where the language is supposed to echo and point to the experiences in question, and a language of explanation. Explanation—within the problematic that Jung is involved within the *Red Book*—is what *kills*. That is what he's been doing up to 1912, and it's left him empty.

JH: Left him personally?

SS: Personally. And God knows what it's done to the people that he's worked with and his associates. Now, the issue then is what is this work? Is this still psychology? This is the problem he struggles with. Ultimately he moves away from the work, back to a form of conceptualism, because he feels that he would lose his scientific credentials if he gave himself over to this form of expression.

JH: Or that the forms he understood, which we were discussing earlier, the forms of what are considered aesthetics in art, during his time, were inadequate and he had in his experience broken through to new forms, but he hadn't formulated them yet, and that's the missing piece. The formulation of the new experience of the soul, without regressing to the old mode of formulation, meaning the conceptual.

SS: And also to what he would call aestheticism, the notion that there is an aesthetics that is merely of the surface or of appearance. There's a deeper sense in which the aesthetic is what one used to convey the depth of the experience, which is the aesthetic that he himself is engaged with and which is in many ways inelegant. This is not a well-written book, nor are the paintings formally realized, but it is more effective precisely for that reason, or it is affective precisely for that reason. It jars with his own category of the aesthetic.

JH: That's right. But the trouble here is that he's still walking around with this split that occurred post-Greek between the aesthetic and the ethical, and therefore if it is only aesthetic it's dilettantish, not truly engaged, and therefore immoral or unethical. That's the aestheticism. But don't forget, that position is already discussed and dealt with by the Romantics, by the Greeks, by the Renaissance, long before, so that Jung is coming out of a tradition—I don't know whether I'd call it Protestantism or what—that has already prejudged the only aesthetic as without moral value.

SS: I think what is critical here, which links to what we were discussing concerning cosmology, is fitting expression, appropriate expression, insightful expression. The language of the *Red Book* is in my view Jung's most insightful, precisely because it is not conceptual. In the second layer, where he reflects on his experience, what he attempts to do is allow the experiences themselves to reverberate, to echo.

JH: That's very important. All language has to shift toward the adjectival and away from the nominative.

SS: When he switches to the nominative, to then explain it through the concept of the shadow, something has gone. The language no longer conveys directly the experience in question.

JH: A universal generic science?

SS: Yes. He's not satisfied with a language that is, one could say, merely insightful, or poignant, or evocative.

JH: Because he still understands psychology in terms of a field of understanding human nature. But suppose psychology were really a practice, not a field of understanding or meaning, but a way, as he so often uses the word. A way of living, a way of seeing, a way of hearing, a way of responding, a way of sensing the Gods in the world, the way the Greeks did when they went to the theater and watched an Aeschylus or a Sophocles play all day long, never to be seen again. Suppose it were not quite the way we've imagined it? As long as we imagined psychology to be an "ology" then we have to find the language for constructing that "ology" and that's very different from psychology as a way. I'm a psychologist, I live the world, what you might say, through the soul. I don't quite know what that is, or what it means, but it saves me from trying to imagine that I'm engaged with understanding the world, and I'm back to what I said earlier about appreciating the world, rather than understanding it. Not a reasoned world but a beautiful world. And what happens then to the way you are in the world, and with the world.

SS: This connects with another aspect in the *Red Book* at this point, which is an affirmation of life. Appreciation is clearly another mode of expressing the affirmation of life, the acceptance of existence in all its forms.

JH: That's extremely important, because that touches on the Job question, and Abraxas, and the nature of Christ as also embracing the evil principle.

SS: He has to find, which he does, a dark language. There is a gruesomeness, there is blood, but he has to accept that. He realizes this is part of existence, that it has to be welcomed, it has to be contended with, and language was one of the means to do that. Also for him painting and, indeed, sculpting.

JH: Even architecture. For the person living in the Western tradition, as I am, and as I imagine is everybody who's engaged with this book, there's that wonderful French sentence "*comprend tout, ça veut dire pardonner tout,*" you can excuse everything that exists once you understand it. It belongs, you would say. No Manichaeism, it all belongs. Everything is for the best in this best of all possible worlds. *Candide.*[145] If you take that position, according to the Western moralists of our major tradition, you've ignored again the importance of the ethical, and that understanding requires discrimination, and seeing the better from the worse, and standing for the better against the worse, etc. That's always going to come up, isn't it? Even if you say affirmation of life and acceptance and even celebration, it's still going to come up that you've ignored something, you've let something slip away that is very important for the human soul, a certain ethical and moral position.

SS: Within that sense, part of what Jung contends with is the notion of the irrationality of the real, that there is a *ratio* that can be understood, and from early on in the text he contends with the fact that much of life is incomprehensible. There's the craziness, there's the madness that runs in the streets, and that too has to be accepted. Not simply to be comprehended one day when our science is good enough. One has to find the right comportment toward it in the present.

JH: Which makes it neither rational nor irrational. It simply *is*.

SS: It *is* part of what exists, so that, as I understand it, the ethics come in the attitudes one takes, how one positions oneself toward what exists. In this regard he sees the way that he has shunned so much of existence as the problem. That is, in that sense, unethical.

JH: Good, yes. That would be his confinement, the Jung of the "I," big letter Ego, "I."

SS: His ideals. His quest for the good has created this vast domain that he has shunned. It has been violent in what it has shoved to one side. It's not a question then of simply a reversal of values, of giving himself over, of celebrating in the other side or giving up the good. No, it's one of recognizing its consequences, the consequences of his actions.

JH: And also what you've just said, all that he's shunned. He's created a vast realm of violence and devilry. It's a huge self-examination of what has conditioned him, and it's part of understanding human history, part of understanding what the dead are complaining about, why they haven't been let in.

SS: For himself, again early on, he realizes what he's shunned is pleasure. He's shunned the little things, he's shunned the everyday, and realizes that this too is part of what exists. He's not going to ascend if he doesn't take cognizance of this. But he's not saying that this is true of everyone. These are the consequences of the way he's lived his life and the ideals he's followed.

JH: This life affirmation is not the way it so often sounds in new-age degenerations of that idea, or the reversal of all values. For him it's a wrestling and he has to wrestle with the very "I" that is committed to this. He has to continually go through a shrinking. The affirmation of life isn't a blind thing, it's a shrinking of how little you know, how you cannot avoid your own mistakes.

SS: It's a humbling experience.

JH: Yes, a humbling experience.

SS: His "I" is reduced down to size, where he realizes the scope of life.

THIRTEENTH CONVERSATION

JH: I have a personal question, so let's just touch on it. You told me that some years back you were into psychology, and then you left it or it left you, and in my case I never really left it. But I got into it differently. Maybe because I was writing. I was trying to write a very complex novel in my twenties, based on complicated characters who become each other, very complex, way beyond my ability. But I was aimed at writing, and I lived in Ireland and the whole writing world. Well I didn't have it, I didn't feel I had it. I didn't have the fire in the belly for writing, or I wasn't original, or I was too afraid, or I was too derivative, or who knows what. But there was something else that drew me that wasn't what I was doing, which was writing. What it turned out to be was the understanding of human nature, which I was trying to get at in these very complicated writing pieces. So psychology was the way to get at what I was really interested in underneath, which I think was covered over by writing, because to write you have to love stories and I was not that interested in stories.

SS: I also wrote, but I wrote poems, not stories, and that was prior to my interest in psychology. I wrote and I painted for a few years, but I found it no longer contained me. I got drawn into a fascination with dreams, with understanding. I remember there was one point where I did a painting, and then directly afterward I wrote an attempt at a phenomenological study of the actual process of doing the painting, stroke by stroke, which was fairly absurd!

JH: No, that's interesting. It's really Jung's question, How do you make religion, how do you make a painting?

SS: I got more interested in the process of inspiration rather than the end product. So that was then a shift toward psychology. My interest in your writings was that for the first time I saw an interest, a taking up, of Jung's work that was not antiaesthetic, that didn't have a complete distance from what I was interested in.

JH: I always thought that psychology goes on in the writing. So one of the questions I used to ask myself was how do you write psychology? Well, you must write it so that it touches the soul, or it's not psychology. It has to have that moving quality of experience, and that means it has to have many sorts of metaphors and absurdities and things that go with life. Otherwise you're writing an academic or a scientific description of something but it's no longer psychology.

SS: Put it that way, it strikes one as obvious, in the sense that to express the complexities of life you need to use the full range of the instrument. You need all the keys of the piano and you need all the shadings, all the colorings. It's then absurd to think you could do that on a restricted keyboard, which is conceptual language.

JH: A very narrow keyboard. When you began to be interested in dreams, were you interested in working out your own nature? I wasn't. I think I was entangled in self-understanding, but I don't think that my interest in psychology or even in Jung was to figure myself out, and that continues for me today.

SS: My interest was exploration, is the way I'd put it. It wasn't simply a question of staring into my own entrails, but to understand, at that stage, dreams. Not just my own but dreams themselves. That struck me as the larger quest. I still think it's a great challenge, an open challenge, to understand life in the way we were talking about, without appeal to transcendence, without starting from an axiomatic basis.

JH: The only axiomatic basis I have is that we are lived by powers we pretend to understand, so the axiomatic basis are these powers. They're our mysteries, they're our figures, they are occasions of invasion and they are our lives, or at least determine our lives in strong ways. So those are, you might call, transcendent axiomatic forces.

SS: I moved away from psychology because the whole field looked like a Babel of competing tongues. If you take, for instance, the quest for a science of psychology, after a hundred years is there a single law that psychologists would agree upon?

JH: That's because even some psychologists don't admit the unconscious, which is sort of fundamental.

SS: I got rid of that concept as well. I found I lived much better without it. But then I didn't just move away from psychology, I got interested in the psychology-making process, which is in a way still a psychological question. If the aim to understand human beings hasn't seemed to have reached the resolution that people intended at the beginning of the twentieth century, can we at least study this subset of human beings called psychologists? Can we look at how they function, how they put together these works, what they were intending to do? My interest then is taking psychologies apart and putting them back together to see how they are made. And you can't use psychology to do that, because then you're in an infinite regress. You can't use psychological categories. That takes you to the question of looking at the projects of human understanding. What were people trying to do, how were they put together, and why didn't they work or why *did* they work in certain ways? How do you assess what they came up with?

JH: The very use of the words "human understanding" brings us to the philosophers who wrote tracts and essays on the inquiry into that very question. How do we understand the human mind and human nature? Our investigation was the province of philosophy. How does psychology get made? How does the logic of the mind work? How do feelings work and what are their relations one with another? That was the subject of *all* the great philosophers, in modern times anyway. Maybe I'm wrong to want to tie it to literature, maybe it should be tied to philosophy, but I don't think so.

SS: It's a question of whether psychology ever managed to separate itself from philosophy.

JH: Well, can it?

SS: I don't think it ever managed to.

JH: And then I wonder why it should. Except that philosophy . . . Oh that's a whole new area, I don't know if I want to go there.

SS: We'll put that on hold.

JH: But the questions that philosophy deals with, how to live, what's a virtuous life, what is evil, etc., are they not psychological questions? Or do psychological questions ask the question, Why does philosophy ask those questions?

SS: The other way of formulating it, the philosopher's riposte, would be what you call psychology as an attempt to answer the classic philosophical question: What is the nature of the good? Or, to take it up from Aristotle, what is weakness of the will? Can one knowingly err? The classic questions from Greek philosophy. What is learning? Or Aristotle's *De Anima*, which you mentioned earlier: What moves the soul? How is it composed?

JH: We'll put that aside.

SS: For me, the study of the history of psychology is an attempt to understand human nature but in an extremely roundabout way. It's to inquire not directly into the subject but into attempts to understand human nature and see what one can learn about human nature from that. In a way, it is quite absurd, but that seemed to me as close as one could get.

JH: At least those theories give a description of their fantasy about human nature, and you can digest that, but whether it's any closer to what is human nature we don't know.

SS: The way I'd see it is not just fantasies, because these became taken on board by vast sectors of the public. So the question shifts away from a human nature out there and attempts to depict it to this impressionable malleability, the sense in which the question then is not, for instance, in relation to psychoanalysis, whether or not there is an Oedipus complex, but the fact that thousands have scripted their life according to this narrative. That has been the indubitable fact of their existence. The question then is these concepts of psychology *have* created new realities.

JH: Yes, this is the folk psychology in a way, isn't it?

SS: It's given rise to new forms of life. The question is not whether the unconscious exists or not. The question is hundreds and thousands of people have an unconscious and billions don't. I'd be interested in, you could say, an anthropology of the unconscious. Do those who have an unconscious have better lives, are they happier, or what? A comparative study of different forms of psychological existence. It's reintroducing the question of value.

JH: That's interesting. But there's a trap in that too. They've done that with religions. Does one have a happier life if one believes . . . to what extent does one believe, and so on. But to introduce the question of value has been covered over by the science. This isn't a matter of value at all, it is a matter of evidence, of fact, to prove the unconscious.

SS: In my own life, I've felt that the conceptuality of the psychologies that I was using were impoverishing life. It was acting as if something needed to be interpreted and was not already full of significance.

JH: You began to feel that yourself, personally?

SS: Yes.

JH: That's the crucial thing. In the realm of psychotherapy few people do get to that point, as far as I know. They still wait for their interpretation to give significance. A translation into a concept of some sort.

SS: It assumes that what is there is insufficient on its own terms, that it requires something put into it, such as hermeneutics or signification.

JH: But we've talked a lot about that. What we haven't really been fair to, it seems to me, is the universality that Jung is trying to get at. Despite all his caveats and cautions, about not taking what I've written here as the truth for you, personally, or that this is only one man's journey, is his intense desire to formulate some kind of satisfactory Christianity. I don't know if you think that way, but I think this permeates the *Red Book*, that he's terribly dissatisfied with Christianity and sees all that it's done to him and the world and history and the dead. And on the other hand, he's not willing to let it go and wants to reimagine it, let's say.

SS: He wants to revive the spirit of the early Church.

JH: Revive the inner spirit of the early Church based on internal symbol formation, actual living experience?

SS: Yes. Before, as he expresses it in the Polzeath seminars, it was "snuffed out by ecclesiastical Christianity," by the institution.[146]

JH: In that sense he belongs to the true believers in the early Church. That was genuine revelation.

SS: Yes, there was a revelation. And there was the possibility of it happening to an individual, or an individual experiencing that revelation.

JH: Why shouldn't we follow this and say that's what Jung has come to through this tremendous work? Not just the *Red Book* but things that happened thereafter. And why shouldn't we say that's the religion, the religious answer that he's come up with, and why shouldn't we all follow it? He's found the answer.

SS: He found the answer for himself, and he found the answer for a number of people. The questions that engaged him were to what extent was what he'd come up with iterable, to what extent was it individual and unique, and to what extent did it have wider significance? Could he lead another to this same affirmation of existence that he himself had experienced, to the same depth of religious experience?

JH: And there he stays in the tension.

SS: Yes. I don't think this is a question that's resolved. I don't think he ever comes down on one side or the other on this. One way to take this up is to say, for Jung, the questions are framed in religious language. If one refers, for instance, to his understanding of the predicament in the West, such as in his text from the 1950s *Present and Future*, in a chapter called "Religion as a Counter to Mass-Mindedness," there is the sense that there had been a process of secularization, which had had certain catastrophic effects, in the loss of meaning, the great neurosis of our time.[147] These are familiar tropes of Jung's sociohistorical critique, the solution then formulated in terms of individual religious experience. But if one stops for one minute and asks if that process of supposed secularization actually had been a problem, why does the recovery of meaning need to be framed in religious terms?

JH: Yes, why does it? Why can't it be framed in evolutionary terms or something else?

SS: Without a recourse to that language and the baggage that comes with it.

JH: But not for Jung. It is framed in religious terms.

SS: I recall a work by a man named Tim Fitzgerald called *The Ideology of Religious Studies*.[148] It began with a very provocative thesis where he is simply stating that the term "religion" has become completely meaningless as an analytic category, that it no longer demarcates anything specific, and that it is itself of recent invention. He argues it's precisely within the context of Max Mueller's project of comparative religions that a concept of religion becomes developed, which in itself is framed on the basis of Judeo-Christianity and which then gets expanded, universalized, to encapsulate practices and conceptions in other historical epochs. So it's one of these words where in any conversation no two people actually mean the same thing when they're talking about it. "Religion" has become a symbolic term.

JH: When we say Jung formulates, or finds the way to formulate, what he's working at, he's using religious terms or the history of religion rather than some other path to find meaning, some other category, some other study. I used the word "evolution." Jung means by religion *the tradition*. He uses the early Church, he uses the gnostics, he uses early Christianity, he uses St. Thomas, and so on and so forth, so he is in fact using religion in its historic sense, the passing on of the Christian credo. So he hasn't left that, he hasn't been willing to take up meaning in any other form, as the giving of meaning. It's the religious instinct that counts.

SS: That is privileged in Jung.

JH: It's privileged?

SS: Yes. As you say, you look at the references. I saw the other day there were over a hundred references to Augustine.

JH: That matters in his arguments.

SS: Compare it to the paucity of his references to Shakespeare.

JH: Of course I don't want to go back to literature as a better study. But there's not much Jesus Christ in Shakespeare!

SS: I want to return to this question of why you stayed in psychology. My sense is that when you use the word it's an aspirational term.

JH: Yes.

SS: You still have a dream of psychology, of what it could be.

JH: Yes I do. I've no idea what that is. Maybe there's this great romantic dream of the restoration of the Gods, the return of the romantic vision of Shelley, of Heine in a way, of Nietzsche in a way, of a world in which everything is psychological because everything is metaphorical and mythical. There's no split-off fallen world, in other words, this is a redemptive fantasy. It probably moves me, despite my skepticism. I think it's, as you say, aspirational. In a way it's more than aspirational, it's a very enlivening fantasy. It's like D. H. Lawrence, seeing how alive the world can be, even *is*. At the same time, I'm much more pessimistic than most other people I know. This is nothing I believe but it feeds my own thought.

SS: Losing the sense of aspiration for psychology was what took me out of it. I lost the hope that I would somehow be able to solve things where no one else had. That began to strike me as absurd, so I then turned to rummage within the cemeteries of past psychologies.

JH: You don't need that kind of aspiration. You must have an aspiration, of some sort, within the history of discovery.

SS: In a way, reflecting on it as we're speaking, part of what took me to psychology is still present there, even though it's no longer called psychology.

JH: That's good. That's what *has* you, even though it's no longer officially psychology. But that's partly because psychology's gone to pieces. It's not because *you* left *it*. It left you, and the search is still, in a strange way, for what makes it work, what makes the psyche work.

SS: And I'm fascinated with it. I'm not interested in any other area of historical inquiry.

JH: That's interesting, that sentence. I don't think that would be admitted by historians generally, that their interest is in the deeper subject of their historical search rather than just "doing" history.

SS: To me, it's a question of having sufficient distance to encounter the phenomena at a different level. So then, for instance, I wrote at length about the history of dreams, purely because of my fascination with dreams, but then writing it gave me a new perspective on my own life and on how dreams became seen as disclosive of subjectivity. How I'd come to frame myself, or understand my own dreams, in a certain way. How I'd been taken by the subject so that in a way the process of self-understanding is still there, but in a very indirect way, when it tries to understand the formation of contemporary dream cultures. How they arise, how they form, how they mutate.

There is self-understanding in a tangential or peripheral way but that is nonetheless interesting.

JH: If what is understood in self-understanding is my deep, personal history, that's one thing, it is a disclosure of all that, but if self-understanding is implied by the individual symbol formation that's going on in all these figures and voices, then that's self-disclosure without me in it and, in a strange way, quite different.

SS: It relates to what we were discussing about the dead, in that one has come to think in certain ways through historical evolution that can be traced. What I take as my immediate certitudes, what I take as the givens, are not such, but have arisen through complex and fascinating journeys in the history of ideas—to use Whitehead's expression, of adventures.[149] Some of the greatest adventures of Western thought. Undertaking that work desolidifies one's own certitudes, or what one takes as givens, and I think it also frees one to think of things in new ways. In this sense I consider historical study as a form of prophylactic skepticism.

JH: Prophylactic skepticism? That's all right. It also puts salt on the bird of aspirations.

SS: Which stings sometimes.

JH: Which stings and is all right. Without the skepticism you're just a fool. One of the great things you get from Jung, after all this knowledge, and all this study, and all these languages and readings and footnotes, is that we don't really know very much about life!

SS: There's a marvelous sentence where he says our knowledge of the mind is akin to our knowledge of natural history in the thirteenth century.[150] At another point, in *Mysterium Coniunctionis*, he says when they come back and look at our stuff and what we're writing about, they will wonder and think we're as clueless as were the alchemists as to what we were up to.[151]

JH: Oh I think so, yes, with very obscure language.

FOURTEENTH CONVERSATION

SS: One of the most striking things about the *Red Book* when one first encounters it is the extent and the character of Jung's involvement with Christianity. The central character of the work is Christ. And what is striking in comparison to the other personages is Christ is not interpreted as an aspect of his personality. It's in the work and yet the theological or metaphysical ground is there in a way that is not the case with any of the other personages.

JH: He's still the unpsychologized Christ.

SS: Yes, it's the one figure that is not psychologized.

JH: Now, he talks, this Christ, I'm trying to remember where.

SS: He appears in the closing sequence of *Scrutinies*, as the blue shade, who makes the parting statement of the book: "I bring you the beauty of suffering,"[152] which is required for he who welcomes, or allows in, the Worm, namely Satan.

JH: Allows in the Worm?

SS: Yes. Satan. The question throughout the work is: What does it mean to be a Christian? How is one to understand the imitation of Christ today and does it have any meaning? It's Jung's attempt to recover a genuine experience of being a Christian.

JH: But the Christ then is a particularly described Christ, if it's emphasizing the beauty of acceptance of suffering, acceptance of the Worm. This is not a militaristic Christ—there are endless Christs, or the one who redeemed the world and so on, it's not even the forgiving Christ—it's the accepting or, as you said, life-affirming Christ.

SS: With an unexpected teaching, namely the beauty of suffering. The implication is that it is what one has to learn, given that one is allowing in the Worm, in other words, that one is accepting the horror, the ugliness of existence. One has to be able to perceive the beauty in the suffering.

JH: That would be the counterpart to it. If it's only accepting Abraxas as the evil that's implied with Christ, this is different. This brings an entire other wrapping to it. It seems to come from Jung's long encounter. He doesn't start off with that. He's lost his soul.

SS: But his soul brings him back to Christ. And ultimately I don't think he ever veers from that.

JH: The important thing here for me is that this Christ is a different one from the many, many different kinds of Christ. That's the one we should try to make something of now, in understanding the *Red Book* in terms of Christianity. It's a Christianity that enobles and is arrived at through pain and suffering, through all the encounters, all the learning, that makes him see the particular quality of Christ that is valid, needed, for the Christian today. Would you agree with this, that it's because of the work that he comes to this Christ?

SS: It is. There's an echo for me of Guillaume Apollinaire's magnificent poem "Zone."[153] It has an ending that is the epitome of modernity. It ends with a sequence where he comes to realize these African sculptures, all the novelty, all the exoticism, is but Christ in another form. Written in a similar time. There's a sense in which Jung needed to go out in order to come back. He needed the foray into comparative religion to refind that Christ.

JH: He also had to encounter the figures, who taught him a lot and put him through a lot of suffering, until he discovered this Christ in the beauty of the suffering, but he had to go through *something*.

SS: He had to undergo the experience.

JH: That's what I'm thinking. Maybe that's why he says his book is not everybody's book, or a message for everyone, because you couldn't just pick up that Christ and realize, aha, that's the message, that's the Christ for our day, who understands the beauty of suffering and who can incorporate the Worm because that's copping out of the experience that led to the awareness. It had to come from Jung's own individual symbol formation, I would think. This is not a dogmatic figure.

SS: It clearly has to be out of his own direct experience, also limned against the context he finds himself in. I imagine him at this time reading the *Neue Zuercher Zeitung* every morning, with the brutal atrocities of the war on a daily basis. This is what he's also confronting, not simply his own experience, but trying to find a way in which he can remain in and accept the world he's in. This is the life that he's attempting to affirm—not simply his own well-being but how to affirm being in this world and accepting this as part of existence.

JH: That's a very good insight. It becomes very much experiential rather than, as I said, dogmatic or theological or all the other things that get in the way, so much of the historical Christ, in the folk mind. And I suppose you would say he connects this Christ of today, which he's discovered, with the early Church, where love was such an important concern, and the early fathers. This book becomes an instrument that the various Christian churches should take up and enjoy. It's a new revelation, as has been said, or a new dispensation.

SS: I somehow don't think they're going to see it like that!

JH: Since the beginning of Jung's presentation of his ideas in the 1920s, I think the Christian world took to Jung very quickly and many of the people who promoted Jung in the world were active Christians.

SS: That's true.

JH: And I think that's always been there, and it's one of my objections to that pious aspect of Christianity, and the reinterpretation of Jung's insights into constant redemptive moves without a real grasp of the horror, the horror, as Conrad said. Jung grasped the horror, but I don't think the Christian followers have, and there are a hell of a lot of them. They just have the same pattern of redemption, you know, there's light at the end of the tunnel, forever—you really are redeemed. You see, one thing about Jews, we've not been redeemed. Christ died for our sins. God gave his only blessed, beloved son, you know. That's Christian. You're already saved. Christ has already saved you. There's a place waiting for you in heaven. This is unacceptable to a Jewish mind. There's too much trouble, too much horror. You can't get away with it so easily. I'm not saying that the Christians themselves get away with it so easily, or that Jung did in what you've just described. I *am* saying that the pseudo-Christianity of Jungianism does, and that's part of my fury. I wrote an awful lot of chapters in other books—one chapter is called "A Running Engagement with Christianity"[154]—but my reason for that is because it's destructive to psychology, to the reality of the psyche, the way the soul really is. Jung in his old age had to deal with religion, as if this is the big block, and he wrote *Job*.[155] Freud in his old age wrote *The Future of an Illusion*,[156] and other things that dealt with religion, and was powerfully antireligion. Lacan said if religion wins, psychoanalysis is finished, meaning there's no place in the world for both honest psychoanalysis, honest psychology that sees things as they are, and the pious hypocrisy of Christianity as it's been handed down to us for two thousand years. And that's my objection. I'm not against Christianity in its doctrinal, mythical, inventive, theological basis. I think it's amazing what Christian theology has invented, amazing also how fertile it is for the arts and for so much else. Part of which, its fertility, resides not in these doctrines but in the absurdity of the doctrines, that Jesus is an impossibility as a God and a man, so you already have a mythical figure. The fact of elevating a mythical figure to the heights, to the truth, is a fantastic revelation, which the Christians themselves have missed.

SS: There's a statement attributed to Tertullian that Jung cites approvingly in various contexts: "I believe because it's absurd" or, more accurately, "The Son of God died, which is immediately credible because it is absurd. And buried, he rose again, which is certain because it is impossible."[157]

JH: Because it's absurd. Yes. And the fact that it's absurd makes it acceptable only on the level of imagination. This implies that the central figure in Christianity is mythical, as this is a biological impossibility. So the believing Christians are believing in an image. The great Christian interpreters that I admire are people such as Blake, who take Christ *as* the imagination. But that's a very different Christianity.

SS: That is what Jung is attempting to restore.

JH: Maybe.

SS: Part of what you call the pious pseudo-Christianity of the Jungians partly came about, I think, because they read his late works on Christian dogma, on ritual and symbolism, without seeing the figural ground and understanding the nature of his engagement with it. It's precisely because Jung thinks that ecclesiastical Christianity has killed Christianity. It's precisely because its effects have been so catastrophic that he engages with these texts. So it's on the basis of an absolutely withering critique that he takes up these particular aspects, to try to find something in it. Again, for a Protestant to write about the Mass is a pretty peculiar thing.

JH: And the Trinity. When I'm talking about the Christians, I'm not only talking about those who are denominationally officially Christian, or go to church or whatever. We're all Christians. We're all suffering the two-thousand-year curse that has been laid on us by what you all like so much, the early Church. As Jung explains to the "Red One," his devil, in the *Red Book*, "Do you believe that Christianity left no mark on the souls of men?"[158] Don't forget what the early Church did, a lot of murder, a lot of victimization too. But you don't have murderers unless you have martyrs. So the enjoyment of martyrdom is all part of the same sadism.

SS: And destruction of learning and of culture.

JH: I'm afraid I would be with Emperor Julian until he died, and a lot of these other strange Romans who wouldn't give up the old religion. But I wouldn't take the old religion as they did. In fact if I return to the Greeks and the Romans, the whole movement was not to restore the old religion, that is, we all have to worship the Gods and all that stuff. It's to restore the mythical, the fact that none of it is real or true. These are stories on which everything is based. Wonderful fictions, articulated by some of the most extraordinary writers and dramatists ever, and sculptors too.

SS: There's a point in the *Red Book* when Jung realizes it's only by treating them as fantasy that the Gods have been preserved.[159]

JH: He says that? Exactly. Why didn't I read that book years ago? And they also have not just been preserved but they fertilize, and they go on fertilizing.

Well now, have we done justice to this basic, crucial, central aspect of the *Red Book*? And now comes the question, Sonu, of psychology after the *Red Book*, incorporating the idea that Christ is the central figure of the *Red Book*. Where do Christ and Christianity fit into a new psychology?

SS: Well, it's the central figure for Jung. It's the central figure in his personal iconography, but also, as you say, for much of Western culture, given the effects that Christianity has had, as Jung says in the work, upon the soul.

JH: Exactly. In that sense, we've all been baptized. Our pagan sins have been washed from us. Or the sin of paganism has been washed from us.

SS: But there's a countermovement that he articulates in the work. To quote Lewis Mumford's phrase in his review of *Memories, Dreams, Reflections*, "the revolt of the demons."[160] It is also the return of paganism.

JH: Oh absolutely. And a large part of the dead are the pagans, wouldn't you think?

SS: Yes. It is an acknowledgment of those dead and their lament. And it's a Christianity that becomes repaganized, the figure of Abraxas, the uniting of the Christian God with Satan. This is a truly monstrous image in the full sense of the word. It's completely heretical. Or the God that is reborn in Jung's soul, on the one hand echoing Eckhart's continuing rebirth of God in the soul, is also Abraxas, the son of the earth, the son of the frogs. Jung's theophany brings the pagan and the Christian together, with an admixture of Hinduism to spice up the brew, when the soul becomes refigured as Kali.

JH: I'm wondering how theologians, Christian writers, have responded to the *Red Book*. I don't mean the public that's bought it, or the Jungians that have organized it. There must be some first-rate scholars of Christianity, some thinkers, who have something to say about this, as a massive assault and deeply pious piece of work. Has there been any such response?

SS: I heard that the pastor who gave the oration at Jung's funeral, in which he described Jung as a heretic, was still alive past the age of one hundred, and he read the work and was planning to write something about it, but then died. I would love to have heard what he had to say about it.

JH: But where are all the scholars of the early Church? Just the Christian writers and professors who went to Eranos, there was always one or two, they would have things to say today about this. I'm wondering who's saying something.

SS: It's a great question. I haven't heard any echoes as yet.

JH: Because the reviews in the newspapers are ridiculous. They don't really go at it. They're still worried about whether Jung was a nut or not. It's ridiculous. But the substance that we're talking about, are they letting that all just go by?

SS: I think in the public response, largely, yes. Or they're swallowing it, without knowing what they've swallowed. Many people have been taken by the allure of the images, the exoticism of the work, the sense of mana that emanates from it, without yet stopping to read it, so in a way its true effects have yet to begin.

JH: You're right, it is only a year or two. Very little time.

Connecticut

FIFTEENTH CONVERSATION

SS: We are returning to the question of a new psychology. Rather than attempting to establish a new psychology to replace what has been, which would be an enormous task, an alternative would be simply to state that what is required is to view the old psychology in a new way, to reconsider it, to reconceive what it has been, what it has done, and how it has functioned. What do you say to that?

JH: One of the great advantages of this alternative is that you step aside from the usual *puer senex*, new versus old arguments that are a real cliché, and worse it is a silly thing to talk about. What would be a step in that direction?

SS: In a way, what we have been trying to elaborate in these discussions is precisely that, reconceiving what psychology has been.

JH: What it has been—the historian's approach—how it has created what we call psychology.

SS: Yes, as a way to thinking about it differently. I am just wary of the idea that what is required is a new psychology. There is no shortage of psychologies.

JH: It has made a huge worldwide enterprise, spreading continuously, especially Jung's psychology. China, eastern Europe. Psychotherapy of all sorts. So the task would be looking at the present psychology as a product, as a result in a causal sense. I think we've already been doing this, as you said: what you've called the rails. I think the next step in this dialogue has to come from you, because you are the historian. You know what psychology is or has become and I've been in a kind of prophetic mode: what will it be, what is in the cards. I think you can see farther than I can by looking backward, in an old renaissance manner of doings things. By looking backward and around you can do better than merely prophetic ramblings.

SS: That's a difficult question. I tend to separate out considerations of my private cosmology, my private metaphysics, from historical work.

JH: Good. I'll join you in a private cosmology.

SS: For example, music has a far more pivotal place in the pantheon than psychology. But I keep it to myself! However, it does connect to some of the themes we've been discussing, since at a personal level what has been important to me is a practice of trying to attend to things with fewer presuppositions and encrustations. How can I be responsive to what is there and greet it in its strangeness, and also accept the limitation of understanding?

JH: I can hear the voices in the gallery shouting, Oh come on now, lets have some adventurous freedom! Lets risk it. I have risked, already in the last conversations, when I've said the new people who are training to be psychotherapists at least should indulge themselves in the arts, because that's where they can understand, assuming that psychology's task is grappling with the questions of human nature in relation to the world, in relation to history, and in relation to conundra that perplex them about themselves. In other words, their own disturbances. So I've said that for understanding or articulating better who one is, what a human being is, rather than what we already have in psychology we should turn to the arts, for that's where we see how the human being best presents him/herself. I still think that, perhaps even more so. I have to say I am walking on an ice floe, on a sheet of ice in a river in the early spring, as I don't really know much in either direction, whether what was in the past was so bad or what is going on now is. This direction of mine is so promising.

SS: The issue then is not for psychologists to turn to literature and turn it into something like psychology, which would be easy to do, but rather to allow their own endeavor to grapple with the limitation, the pretention of a certain kind of understanding when shown up against the humble respect toward the inexplicableness of human nature as shown in a number of works of great art and literature. That's not well expressed. The issue is one of realizing the limits of understanding.

JH: Jung says the task is bringing the dead to speak. At least we have the same starting point there. Now I found that bringing the dead to speak is both a personal effusion and my dead, in other words, psychology in the old sense. And also bringing the dead to speak in a historical sense, meaning the dead who have been buried in the name of history and by history. By that I mean, "that's past stuff." We don't need to read those things, they belong to the past. Kant has been transcended by Hegel, and so on. So history itself has been part of overcoming, overthrowing of the voices of the past, which Jung says we have to recover and listen to. Now that's a use of history.

SS: Another way to conceive this is that part of "the dead" is the richness of human culture.

JH: Certainly, oh yes. That's one of the reasons I have always put so many footnotes referring to the dead in my books. I have wanted them to speak all through my books. It has been one of my crucial desires. Don't let them die on you. If you can bring someone back to life that's great. At least don't let them die on your watch.

SS: A question in historical work is always who to revive.

JH: That's the big game. The warfare that goes on long after the combatants are dead, so to speak.

SS: And you realize there is a responsibility that goes with it.

JH: Is this like the revival of the pagan Gods? Is that what we are engaged with here? In a Warburg world?

SS: Good question.

JH: What I have wrong with this is a certain academic sterility.

SS: The issue may be not so much one of revival, in the positive sense, that is, to bring it all back into the present, but one of learning to dwell among the shades, of learning to be present in and among what is already here but not in a tangible, visible way.

JH: This touches on the question of literalism, which always engages me and gives me enjoyment. The literalism of bringing them back.

SS: The issue then is saying, well, the dead are already here.

JH: Yes.

SS: And we need to recognize their presence and learn to see them.

JH: And not create a literalism.

SS: Realizing that the task is one of reframing how one sees them and seeing oneself. Relativizing one's present preoccupations by realizing their presence. What one takes to be one's own, what one intensely focuses on, is caught up in this whole maelstrom.

JH: Yes.

SS: In a way, was that not what Jung was trying to evoke in his conceptual work, however adequately, with the word "archetype"? Namely, that what one takes to be new and originary is actually already the echo of an immemorial past, that the present is freighted with memories. I am trying to separate Jung's intuition from his theoretical elaboration, to get at what he was attempting to evoke by speaking in such a way.

JH: Now you see I am less hesitant perhaps than you are, or less wary, because I am already out of the melee. I have descended into the street and come back up! And so I don't need to worry about the cudgels of the enemy. I use the German word *Anliegen*. I have a propensity, I have a feeling for, a calling toward, a sympathy with the sense that this has all not been given before, but yet is always there, and as such conditions *how* I see and feel, *what* I see and feel, how I respond, how I would like to respond: all of that and more, too, that I don't even imagine, is already there in the imagination, and to which I have access through my personal life, that is by digging into my responses and coming up with insights. So if the archetypes are the primordially given, then they are determinants, as Auden says, and I quote him again and again, "We are lived by powers we pretend to understand."[161] We could stop right here.

Notes

1. On this ritual, see http://www.
   digitalegypt.ucl.ac.uk/religion/
   wpr.html.
2. Gilles Deleuze and Félix
   Guattari, *Anti-Oedipus:
   Capitalism and Schizophrenia*,
   tr. Robert Hurley, Mark Seem,
   and Helen Lane (London:
   Continuum, 2004).
3. Hugo Grotius (1583–1645)
   was a Dutch jurist whose work
   was esteemed by the Italian
   philosopher Giambattista
   Vico (1668–1744). On Vico,
   see James Hillman, "Plotino,
   Ficino and Vico as Precursors
   of Archetypal Psychology," in
   *Loose Ends: Primary Papers in
   Archetypal Psychology* (Dallas:
   Spring Publications, 1975),
   pp. 146–79.
4. C. G. Jung, *The Red Book.
   Liber Novus*, edited by Sonu
   Shamdasani, translated by
   Mark Kyburz, John Peck, and
   Sonu Shamdasani (New York:
   W. W. Norton, 2009), p. 294.
5. Ibid., p. 265f.
6. Ibid., p. 235.
7. Ibid., p. 260.
8. William James, *Pragmatism
   and Four Essays from the
   Meaning of Truth* (Cleveland,
   Ohio: Meridian, 1970 [1907]).
   On James, See Rámon del
   Castillo, "The Comic Mind of
   William James," in *William
   James Studies* 8:1, www.
   williamjamesstudies.org/8.1/
   castillo.pdf.
9. Cited in John Edward Hasse,
   *Beyond Category: The Life and
   Genius of Duke Ellington* (New
   York: Da Capo 1993), p. 222.
10. *Red Book*, p. 254.
11. Ibid., pp. 267, 277.
12. Ibid., p. 231.
13. Ibid.
14. Jung, *Visions: Notes of the
    Seminar Given in 1930–1934*,
    ed. Claire Douglas, 2 vols.,
    Bollingen Series (Princeton,
    NJ: Princeton University Press,
    1997).
15. See Jung, "Psychological
    Commentary on the *Tibetan
    Book of the Dead*," *CW* 11;
    *Modern Psychology. Notes
    on the Lectures Given at the
    Eidgenössische Technische
    Hochschule, Zürich by Prof.
    Dr. C. G. Jung, October 1933–
    February 1940*, compiled and
    translated by Elizabeth Welsh
    and Barbara Hannah (Zürich,
    1959, privately published, 2nd

ed.), vols. 3 and 4, p. 153f (ed. Martin Liebscher, Philemon Series, in preparation); *The Psychology of Kundalini Yoga: Notes of the Seminar Given in 1932*, ed. Sonu Shamdasani, Bollingen Series (Princeton, NJ: Princeton University Press, 1996).

16. See Sonu Shamdasani, *C. G. Jung: A Biography in Books* (New York: W. W. Norton, 2012), and Alfred Ribi, "Zum schopferischen Prozess bei C. G. Jung. Aus dem Excerptbänden zur Alchemie," *Analytische Psychologie*, 1982, pp. 201–21.

17. *Red Book*, p. 339.

18. Ibid., p. 231.

19. Ibid., p. 297.

20. Karl Jaspers, *The Perennial Scope of Philosophy*, tr. Ralph Mannheim (London: Routledge, 1950), p. 170. See James Hillman, "Jaspers Attack on Demonology," in *Healing Fiction* (Barrytown, NY: Station Hill, 1983), p. 63f.

21. Matthew 16:23.

22. Miguel de Unamuno, *The Tragic Sense of Life in Men and Nations*, tr. Anthony Kerrigan, Bollingen Series (Princeton, NJ: Princeton University Press, 1972).

23. Ernest Becker, *The Denial of Death* (New York: The Free Press, 1973); Jessica Mitford, *The American Way of Death*

(New York: Simon and Schuster, 1978).

24. *Red Book*, p. 274.

25. Ibid., p. 239.

26. David Farrell Krell, "Immanent Death, Imminent Death: Reading Freud's *Beyond the Pleasure Principle* (1920), with Heidegger's *Being and Time* (1927) and *Metaphysical Foundations of Logic* (1928), though there's Something in it for Aristophanes too . . . ," in Sonu Shamdasani and Michael Münchow, *Speculations After Freud: Psychoanalysis, Philosophy and Culture* (London: Routledge, 1994), pp. 151–66.

27. *Red Book*, p. 297.

28. Ibid., pp. 159, 217.

29. James Hillman, *Re-Visioning Psychology* (New York: HarperCollins, 1975).

30. *Red Book*, p. 200.

31. Mary Watkins, *Waking Dreams* (New York: Harper and Row, 1976).

32. William James, *The Principles of Psychology*, vol. 1 (New York: Henry Holt, 1890), p. 225.

33. Jung, *CW* 5.

34. *Red Book*, p. 245f.

35. Léon Daudet, *L'Hérédo: Essai sur le drame intérieur* (Paris: Nouvelle Librairie nationale, 1916).

36. *Red Book*, p. 267f.

37. Ibid., p. 230.

38. "We are lived by powers we pretend to understand: / They

arrange our loves; it is they who direct at the end / The enemy bullet, the sickness, or even our hand. / It is their tomorrow hangs over the earth of the living / And all that we wish for our friends; but existing is believing / We know for whom we mourn and who is grieving." W. H. Auden, "In Memory of Ernst Toller" (1940).

39. Jung, *Psychological Types* (1921), *CW* 6, § 743.

40. *Red Book*, p. 265f.

41. Ibid., p. 199.

42. Wassily Kandinsky, *Concerning the Spiritual in Art*, tr. M. T. H. Sadler (New York: Dover, 1977).

43. See *Red Book*, p. 204.

44. Audio versions available at http://www.ubu.com/sound/ball.html.

45. See Jung, "Ulysses: A Monologue" and "Picasso," *CW* 15.

46. Barbara Hannah, *Jung: His Life and Work. A Biographical Memoir* (New York: Perigree, 1976).

47. William James, *A Pluralistic Universe* (London: Longmans, Green, 1909).

48. Jung, C. G. (1934). *Modern Psychology. Notes on the Lectures given at the Eidgenössische Technische Hochschule, Zürich by Prof. Dr. C. G. Jung, October 1933– February 1934*, compiled and translated by Elizabeth Welsh and Barbara Hannah (Zürich, 1959), privately published, vol. 1, p. 21f. Ed. Ernst Falzeder, Philemon Series, in preparation.

49. See James Hillman, *The Dream and the Underworld* (New York: Harper and Row, 1979), p. 13f.

50. Aniela Jaffé and C. G. Jung, *Memories, Dreams, Reflections*, tr. Clara and Richard Winston (New York: Vintage, 1962).

51. "Easy is the descent to Avernus: / night and day the door of gloomy Dis stands open; / but to recall your steps and pass out to the upper air, / this is the task, this is the toil." "facilis descensus Averno/ noctes atque dies patet atri ianua Ditis;/ sed revocare gradum superasque evadere ad auras, / hoc opus, hic labor est." Virgil, *Aeneid*, VI, 126– 29, *Psychology and Alchemy* (1944), *CW* 12, p. 39.

52. Jung, "Yoga and the West," *CW* 11.

53. See Shamdasani, *C. G. Jung: A Biography in Books*, pp. 178–87.

54. *Memories, Dreams, Reflections*, p. 192.

55. Alfred Fouillée, *La Psychologie des idées-forces*, 2. vols. (Paris: Alcan, 1893).

56. Friedrich Nietzsche, "Only a Fool, Only a Poet," in *Dithyrambs of Dionysus*, tr.

R. J. Hollingdale (London: Anvil Press, 1984), p. 23f.

57. See Klaus Ottmann, "Spiritual Materiality: Contemporary Sculpture and the Responsibility of Forms," in *Thought Through My Eyes: Writings on Art, 1977–2005* (Putnam, Conn.: Spring Publications, 2006), pp. 183–89.

58. Jung, "Adaptation, Individuation and Collectivity," *CW* 18.

59. Jeffrey Moussaïef Masson, ed., *The Complete Letters of Sigmund Freud to Wilhelm Fliess 1887–1904* (Cambridge, Mass.: The Belknap Press of Harvard University Press, 1985).

60. Jung/Jaffé Protocols, Jung Collection, Library of Congress, p. 169.

61. See Jung to Herbert Read, 2 September 1960, in Gerhard Adler with Aniela Jaffé, eds., *C. G. Jung Letters*, tr. R. F. C. Hull, Bollingen Series (Princeton, NJ: Princeton University Press, vol. 2, 1975), p. 589.

62. Joseph Campbell, *The Hero with a Thousand Faces*, Bollingen Series (Princeton, NJ: Princeton University Press, 1949).

63. Cited in *Red Book*, p. 214.

64. Tina Keller, "C. G. Jung: Some Memories and Reflections," *Inward Light* 35 (Spring 1972), p. 21.

65. *Red Book*, p. 299.

66. James Dreaver, *Dictionary of Psychology* (Harmondsworth: Penguin, 1958).

67. Arthur Kleinman, *The Illness Narratives: Suffering, Healing and the Human Condition* (New York: Basic Books, 1988).

68. See Shamdasani, "The Optional Unconscious," in Martin Liebscher and Angus Nichols, eds., *Thinking the Unconscious: Nineteenth-Century German Thought*, (Cambridge: Cambridge University Press, 2010), pp. 287–96.

69. Jung, "Commentary on 'The Secret of the Golden Flower'" (1929), *CW* 13, § 75.

70. Jung, "The Practical Utility of Dream Analysis" (1931), *CW* 16, § 320.

71. Jung, "On the Psychology of the Child Archetype" (1940), *CW* 9, I, § 271.

72. Hillman, *The Dream and the Underworld*, p. 68f.

73. James Hillman, *Inter-Views: Conversations with Laura Pozzo on Psychotherapy, Biography, Love, Soul, Dreams, Work, Imagination and the State of Culture* (New York: Harper and Row, 1983), p. 75f.

74. *Red Book*, p. 323.

75. Hillman, "An Imaginal Ego," *Inscape* 2, 1970, pp. 2–8.

76. *Red Book*, p. 303.

77. *Eranos Jahrbuch*, 37, 1968, pp. 299–356, revised in *The*

Myth of Analysis: Three Essays in Archetypal Psychology (Evanston: Northwestern University Press), 1972.

78. *Red Book*, p. 317.

79. Umberto Eco, "The Return of the Middle Ages," in *Travels in Hyperreality* (New York: Harcourt, 1986).

80. Henry Corbin, *Avicenna and the Visionary Recital*, tr. Willard Trask, Bollingen Series (New York: Pantheon Books, 1960).

81. *Red Book*, p. 333f.

82. Jung, "Commentary on 'The Secret of the Golden Flower,' " *CW* 13, § 20.

83. *Red Book*, p. 327.

84. Jung, *Introduction to Jungian Psychology: Notes of the Seminar on Analytical Psychology Given in 1925*, original edition, ed. William McGuire, revised edition, ed. Sonu Shamdasani, Philemon Series (Princeton, NJ: Princeton University Press, 2012), p. 34f.

85. See Tina Keller, "Beginnings of Active Imagination. Analysis with C. G. Jung and Toni Wolff, 1915–1928," *Spring: An Annual of Archetypal Psychology and Jungian Thought*, 1982, pp. 279–94, and Wendy Swan, ed., *The Memoir of Tina Keller-Jenny: A Lifelong Confrontation with the Psychology of C. G. Jung*, with a preface by Sonu Shamdasani

(New Orleans: Spring Journal Books, 2011).

86. William James, *The Varieties of Religious Experience*, Centenary Edition, intro. Eugene Taylor and Jeremy Carrette (London: Routledge, 2002), p. 327.

87. Gopi Krishna, *Kundalini: The Evolutionary Energy in Man*, with a psychological commentary by James Hillman (London: Stuart and Watkins, 1970).

88. *Red Book*, p. 336.

89. See Henri Ellenberger's chapter on Jung in *The Discovery of the Unconscious: The History and Evolution of Dynamic Psychiatry* (New York: Basic Books, 1970), p. 657; see also Shamdasani, *Jung Stripped Bare By His Biographers, Even* (London: Karnac Books, 2005), p. 66f.

90. *Red Book*, p. 295.

91. See Samuel Taylor Coleridge, *Biographica Literaria*, chapter 13, "On the Imagination, or Esemplastic Power," in Donald Stauffer, ed., *Selected Poetry and Prose of Coleridge* (New York: Random House, 1951).

92. David L. Miller, "Imaginings No End," *Eranos* 46, 1977 (Frankfurt am Main: Insel Verlag, 1981), p. 486 n. 97.

93. Edward Edinger, *The Creation of Consciousness: Jung's Myth for Modern Man* (Toronto: Inner City Books, 1984).

94. Maurice Blanchot, *The Infinite Conversation*, tr. Susan Hanson (Minneapolis: University of Minnesota Press, 1992), p. 387; see Michel Foucault, "Madness, the Absence of an Oeuvre," in *History of Madness*, ed. Jean Khalfa and tr. Jonathan Murphy and Jean Khalfa (London: Routledge, 2006), pp. 541–49.

95. See note 20, above.

96. *Notes on the Seminar in Analytical Psychology conducted by Dr. C. G. Jung, Polzeath, England, July 14–July 27, 1923*, arranged by members of the class, unpublished.

97. James Hillman, "Jung's Daimonic Inheritance," *Sphinx* 1, 1988, pp. 9–19.

98. Marianne Jehle, ed., *The Jung–Adolf Keller Correspondence*, Philemon Series, forthcoming.

99. Jung, "Transformation Symbolism in the Mass" (1942), *CW* 11.

100. Jung, "Psychological Interpretation of the Dogma of the Trinity" (1942), *CW* 11.

101. *Red Book*, p. 297.

102. Richard Seager, ed., *The Dawn of Religious Pluralism: Voices from the World's Parliament of Religions, 1893* (La Salle: Open Court, 1993).

103. Jung, *Psychology and Religion* (1938), *CW* 11.

104. See Jung, *Answer to Job* (1952), *CW* 11.

105. Jung, "The Relation of Psychotherapy to the Cure of Souls" (1932), CW 11, § 537.

106. *Liber Novus*, p. 387.

107. Steven Wasserstrom, *Religion after Religion: Gershom Scholem, Mircea Eliade and Henry Corbin at Eranos* (Princeton, NJ: Princeton University Press, 1999).

108. Mircea Eliade, *Yoga: Immortality and Freedom*, tr. Willard Trask, Bollingen Series (Princeton, NJ: Princeton University Press, 1969).

109. Henry Corbin, *Avicenna and the Visionary Recital*, tr. Willard Trask, Bollingen Series (Princeton, NJ: Princeton University Press, 1992).

110. William James, *The Will to Believe* (Cambridge, Mass.: Harvard University Press, 1979).

111. *Red Book*, p. 348.

112. Available on YouTube.

113. *Nietzsche's Zarathustra: Notes of the Seminar given in 1934–39*, ed. James Jarrett, Bollingen Series (Princeton, NJ: Princeton University Press, 1988), p. 381.

114. *Red Book*, p. 293.

115. Ximena de Angulo (1952), "Comments on a Doctoral Thesis," in William McGuire and R. F. C. Hull, eds., *C. G. Jung Speaking: Interviews and Encounters*, Bollingen Series (Princeton, NJ: Princeton

University Press, 1977), pp. 202–13.

116. Jung archive, Swiss Federal Institute of Technology, Zurich.

117. James Hillman, "Concerning the Stone: Alchemical Images of the Goal," in *Alchemical Psychology, James Hillman Uniform Edition* 5 (Putnam, Conn.: Spring Publications, 2010), pp. 231–63.

118. See, for example, *The Psychology of the Transference, CW* 16, § 400.

119. Bruno Latour, *Science in Action: How to Follow Scientists and Engineers through Society* (Cambridge, Mass.: Harvard University Press, 1987).

120. Jung, *Children's Dreams: Notes from the Seminar Given in 1936–1940*, Maria Meyer-Grass and Lorenz Jung, eds., and tr. Ernst Falzeder with the collaboration of Tony Woolfson, Philemon Series (Princeton, NJ: Princeton University Press, 2010).

121. Freud, "Analysis of a Phobia in a Five-Year Old child" (1909), *Standard Edition* 10.

122. See Jung, "Address at the Founding of the Jung Institute" (1948), *CW* 18.

123. See Thomas Hakl, *Der verborgene Geist von Eranos: Unbekannte Begegnungen von Wissenschaft und Esoterik*, Bretten, Scienta nova, 2001, and Ricardo Bernadini, *Jung*

a *Eranos: Il progetto della psicologia complessa* (Rome: Franco Angeli Edizioni, 2011).

124. On the rainmaker, see Jung, *Mysterium Coniunctionis, CW* (1955/56) 14, § 604n.

125. Jung (1957), *CW* 10.

126. Friedrich Nietzsche, *Human, All Too Human: A Book for Free Spirits*, tr. R. J. Hollingdale (Cambridge: Cambridge University Press, 1996), § 200, p. 95.

127. *Red Book*, p. 274.

128. Laurens van der Post, *Jung and the Story of our Time* (New York: Vintage, 1977); on this question, see Shamdasani, *Jung Stripped Bare by his Biographers, Even.*

129. R. G. Collingwood, *The Idea of History* (Oxford: Oxford University Press, 1994).

130. James, *The Varieties of Religious Experience: Centenary Edition.*

131. *Introduction to Jungian Psychology*, p. 103.

132. Catherine Elgin and Nelson Goodman, "The Epistemic Efficacity of Stupidity," in Nelson Goodman, *Reconceptions in Philosophy and Other Arts and Sciences* (London: Routledge, 1988).

133. *Red Book*, p. 299.

134. Ibid., p. 296.

135. Jung, "Adaptation, Individuation and Collectivity" (1916), *CW* 18.

136. *Red Book*, p. 293.

137. "Yet we have gone on living, / Living and partly living." A refrain spoken by the chorus in T. S. Eliot's *Murder in the Cathedral*, in *The Complete Poems and Plays* (London: Faber and Faber, 1969), p. 243f.

138. Jung to Kristine Mann, in Gerhard Adler ed. in collaboration with Aniela Jaffé, *C. G. Jung Letters I: 1906–1950* (London: Routledge, 1973), tr. R. F. C. Hull, pp. 357–59. See Sonu Shamdasani, " 'The Boundless Expanse': Jung's Reflections on Life and Death," *Quadrant: Journal of the C. G. Jung Foundation for Analytical Psychology* 38, 2008, pp. 9–32.

139. Alfred North Whitehead, chapter 1, "Importance," *Modes of Thought* (New York: Macmillan, 1938).

140. "Words are chameleons / music has the right to be abstract / the experience that everything is inexplicable leads to the dream / do not explain music / do not explain dreams. / The ungraspable penetrates all / one must know that everything rhymes." Wols, *Aphorisms and Pictures*, tr. Peter Inch and Annie Fatet (London: Arc, 1971).

141. May 5, 2011.

142. Charles Boer and James Hillman, *Freud's Own Cookbook* (New York: Harper, 1985).

143. See Joseph Delboeuf, *Le Sommeil et les rêves et autres textes* (Paris: Fayard, 1993).

144. *Red Book*, p. 212.

145. Voltaire (1759), *Candide and Other Stories*, tr. R. Pearson (Oxford: Oxford University Press, 1998).

146. *Notes on the Seminar in Analytical Psychology conducted by Dr. C. G. Jung, Polzeath, England, July 14–July 27, 1923.*

147. *CW* 10, §505f.

148. Timothy Fitzgerald, *The Ideology of Religious Studies* (Oxford: Oxford University Press, 2000).

149. Alfred North Whitehead, *Adventures of Ideas* (New York: Simon and Schuster, 1933).

150. Jung, "Basic Postulates of Analytical Psychology" (1931), *CW* 8, § 672.

151. Jung, *Mysterium Coniunctionis* (1955/56), *CW* 14, §173.

152. *Red Book*, p. 359.

153. Guillaume Apollinaire, *Zone*, tr. Samuel Beckett (London: Calder, 1972).

154. Hillman, *Inter-Views*, p. 75f.

155. *Answer to Job* (1952), *CW* 11.

156. Freud (1921), *Standard Edition*, vol. 21.

157. *Psychological Types*, *CW* 6, §17.

158. *Red Book*, p. 260.

159. Ibid., p. 283.

160. *The New Yorker*, May 23, 1964.

161. See above, note 38.

Acknowledgments

I would like to express my gratitude to the late James Hillman, for dedicating such precious time to this project: *vale, amicus meus.* This book would not have been possible without the generosity of understanding and facilitation of Margot McLean. Maggie Baron was of constant support. I would like to thank the Hammer Museum for hosting the Los Angeles conversation in association with the exhibition *The Red Book of C. G. Jung: Creation of a New Cosmology,* in turn made possible through the Philemon Foundation, and in particular Nancy Furlotti. Thanks are due to following for the role in the production of this book: Ellie Stuckey for providing her transcription of her video of the Los Angeles conversation; Valery Lyman for recording the Connecticut conversations; Arlen Cooke and Suren Karapetyan for recording the New York conversations; Clare Craig for transcribing the Connecticut and New York conversations; Don Kennison for his fine copy editing; Laura Lindgren for the elegant layouts; Austin O'Driscoll for her assistance; Cohen Carruth, Inc., for the fine index; John Peck for his ever-keen eye; and Jim Mairs, for an ongoing collaboration since 2005, commencing with the *Red Book.*

Sonu Shamdasani

Index